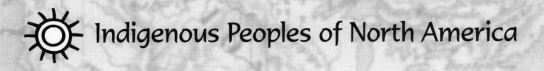
The Cherokee

Cathryn J. Long

Lucent Books, Inc.
P.O. Box 289011, San Diego, California

Titles in the Indigenous Peoples of North America Series Include:

The Apache
The Cherokee
The Iroquois
Native Americans of the Great Lakes
Native Americans of the Northeast
Native Americans of the Plains
Native Americans of the Southeast
Native Americans of the Southwest
The Navajo
The Sioux

Library of Congress Cataloging-in-Publication Data

Long, Cathryn J.
    The Cherokee / Cathryn J. Long
        p.   cm. — (Indigenous peoples of North America)
    Includes bibliographical references (p.   ) and index.
    Summary: Discusses the traditional life of the Cherokee peoples in
the southern Appalachian Mountains, their beliefs and sense of
community, culture, their forced migration along the Trail of Tears
to Oklahoma, and life in the twentieth century and beyond.
    ISBN 1-56006-617-2 (lib. : alk. paper)
    1. Cherokee Indians—Juvenile literature. [1. Cherokee Indians.
2. Indians of North America—Oklahoma. 3. Indians of North America—
Southern States.] I. Title. II. Series.
    E99.C5L65   2000
    975.004'9755—dc21   99-43152
                                                              CIP

Contents

Foreword

North America's native peoples are often relegated to history—viewed primarily as remnants of another era—or cast in the stereotypical images long found in popular entertainment and even literature. Efforts to characterize Native Americans typically result in idealized portrayals of spiritualists communing with nature or bigoted descriptions of savages incapable of living in civilized society. Lost in these unfortunate images is the rich variety of customs, beliefs, and values that comprised—and still comprise—many of North America's native populations.

The *Indigenous Peoples of North America* series strives to present a complex, realistic picture of the many and varied Native American cultures. Each book in the series offers historical perspectives as well as a view of contemporary life of individual tribes and tribes that share a common region. The series examines traditional family life, spirituality, interaction with other native and non-native peoples, warfare, and the ways the environment shaped the lives and cultures of North America's indigenous populations. Each book ends with a discussion of life today for the Native Americans of a given region or tribe.

In any discussion of the Native American experience, there are bound to be similarities. All tribes share a past filled with unceasing white expansion and resistance that led to more than four hundred years of conflict. One U.S. administration after another pursued this goal and fought Indians who attempted to defend their homelands and ways of life. Although no war was ever formally declared, the U.S. policy of conquest precluded any chance of white and Native American peoples living together peacefully. Between 1780 and 1890, Americans killed hundreds of thousands of Indians and wiped out whole tribes.

The Indians lost the fight for their land and ways of life, though not for lack of bravery, skill, or a sense of purpose. They simply could not contend with the overwhelming numbers of whites arriving from Europe or the superior weapons they brought with them. Lack of unity also contributed to the defeat of the Native Americans. For most, tribal identity was more important than racial identity. This loyalty left the Indians at a distinct disadvantage. Whites had a strong racial identity and they fought alongside each other even when there was disagreement because they shared a racial destiny.

Although all Native Americans share this tragic history they have many distinct differences. For example, some tribes and individuals sought to cooperate almost immediately with the U.S. government while others steadfastly resisted the white presence. Life before the arrival of white settlers also varied. The nomads of the Plains developed altogether different lifestyles and customs from the fishing people of the Northwest coast.

Contemporary life is no different in this regard. Many Native Americans—forced onto reservations by the American government—struggle with poverty, poor health, and inferior schooling. But others have regained a sense of pride in themselves and their heritage, enabling them to search out new routes to self-sufficiency and prosperity.

The *Indigenous Peoples of North America* series attempts to capture the differences as well as similarities that make up the experiences of North America's native populations—both past and present. Fully documented primary and secondary source quotations enliven the text. Sidebars highlight events, personalities, and traditions. Bibliographies provide readers with ideas for further research. In all, each book in this dynamic series provides students with a wealth of information as well as launching points for further research.

At the Stomp Ground

Late on a Saturday afternoon, people are arriving at a shady spot deep in the hills of northeastern Oklahoma. Trucks and cars pull off the road and stop under the trees; families spill out, carrying aluminum folding chairs and coolers of food and drink. While the women set up the food under sheds around a flat clearing, the children scurry around their elders. A few teenagers gather to organize a game. At first glance, this could be an average family or community picnic. The people are dressed like any western Americans, with a good scattering of cowboy hats. The young people tease each other, drink sodas, and talk about the latest TV shows.

As dusk falls, though, the feeling changes. At the center of the clearing, a four-log fire has been carefully laid, a log pointing in each of the four directions of the compass. Around the ground, families seat themselves in seven clan groups, according to their ancestry. Then the fire is lit. A man steps out and begins to sing a deep and solemn chant, calling the men and women to dance. A line of people begins to circle the fire; the men sing in response to the leader, while the women set the rhythm by stomping their cowboy boots, which have pebble-filled tortoise shells sewn to the tops. As the hours pass, dance follows dance, the fire crackles, the song and soft, unified thud of feet on the stomp ground become hypnotic. They go on all night, celebrating the glory of the sun, the bounty of harvest, the qualities of plants and animals, and the spirits of their Cherokee ancestors.

The People Who Call Themselves Cherokee

Over 308,000 people identified themselves in the 1990 census as members of the Cherokee tribe, making it the largest tribal group in the United States. The Cherokee make up 16 percent of all Native Americans. About 170,000 Cherokee tribespeople are concentrated in northeastern Oklahoma, where they have no reservation but belong to the federally recognized Cherokee Nation. Another 12,000 or so in the Eastern Band live on or near a reservation next to Great Smoky Mountains National Park in North Carolina. The rest are scattered around the United States.

The reason for their dispersal lies in their long history. Once a powerful tribe in the southeast, they flourished through the early years of U.S. history because of their ability to adapt and organize. Yet their wealth and strength could not protect them from the policy of Indian removal, which forced them west along the "Trail of Tears" in 1838. A few managed to stay in their mountain homeland and became the nucleus of today's Eastern Band. The rest rebuilt in Oklahoma, only to be ruined again by the Civil War and then by a government policy that took land ownership from the tribe. Yet once again, the Cherokee tribe reemerged. Wilma Mankiller, Principal Chief of the Cherokee Nation in the early 1990s, explains their story this way:

> We are a revitalized tribe. After every major upheaval, we have been able to gather together as a people and rebuild a community and a government. Individually and collectively,

Wilma Mankiller, a leader of the Cherokee Nation in the early 1990s.

Cherokee people posess an extraordinary ability to face down adversity and continue moving forward. We are able to do that because our culture, though certainly diminished, has sustained us since time immemorial. The Cherokee culture is a well-kept secret.[1]

What Makes a Person Cherokee

Cherokee culture has always allowed intermarriage, considering children of Cherokee mothers to be full Cherokee. Some of the oldest names among the Cherokee are the names of European traders and pioneers who took Cherokee wives: Adair, Rogers, Ross, Hicks. Even the chief who fought removal in the 1830s was just one-eighth Cherokee by blood. Because of the mixing, many Cherokee do not look very "Indian." Some, today as in the past, have been eager to live just as other Americans do. But many others feel strongly that their Cherokee heritage should play a major part in their lives.

The people at the stomp ground know varying amounts about Cherokee culture. A few of the older people may remember all the old myths and may have read histories. To some of the young, Cherokee ways may simply be their family customs and stories. For everyone at the stomp dance, though, Cherokee identity is repeated and renewed by the physical, ritual movements, and by the sounds and sights of the other dancers in the firelight. In the dance, they feel their connection with the ongoing cycle of generations.

Chapter 1

Traditional Life in the Mountains

Nugatsa'ni: a high ridge with a long gradual slope. *Gadalu'tsi:* a fringe of forest trees standing erect on the horizon. *Gunun'dale'gi:* one who follows the ridge. Words such as these are plentiful in the Cherokee language and carry with them whole pictures. They suggest the origin of the language and its first speakers: the deep wilderness of the southern Appalachian Mountains. The huge area where the Cherokee originally lived and hunted includes land in what is now part of the states of North and South Carolina, Georgia, Alabama, Kentucky, and Tennessee. This land helped determine ways of living and thinking that remain the backbone of Cherokee identity today.

Into the Ancient Landscape

The kind of country inhabited by the people who lived on the continent before Europeans arrived has all but vanished. Visitors to the southern Appalachian region today will see modern farms, highways, shopping malls, factories, and towns. Part of the land has been preserved in the Great Smoky Mountains National Park, and a small portion next to the park is now a reservation for a few thousand members of the Eastern Band of Cherokee Indians. Yet even the park and the reservation have been lumbered and changed by modern development. Rivers have been redirected and dammed. Only small areas remain where an adventurer might look for the true environment of the early Cherokee.

One person who has tried such an adventure, Christopher Camuto, talks of walking through a section of old-growth forest where enormous trees tower over rich patches of varied plants:

> the trail was half above and half below the forest, clinging to a steep pitched slope wet with spring water. Huge poplars and hemlocks dominated the scene, overshadowing a complex assemblage of northern red oak and beech, sugar maple and red maple and mountain silverbell, magnolia and pawpaw—a hemisphere's

The Oconaluftee River in the Cherokee tribal lands of the Great Smoky Mountains National Park, North Carolina.

worth of tree species brought together by terrain and weather and time. Forge Creek made a pronounced bend here and stepped, in its graceful turn, up through long, crescent-shape pools dark with the possibility of trout. Somewhere below me, hidden under a dense picket of rhododendron, laurel, and . . . wild fern, was the confluence of Ekaneetlee Branch and Forge Creek, where an old Cherokee path [went].[2]

As Camuto discovered, Cherokee country was one of eastern North America's most beautiful and biologically diverse places, rich in many kinds of plants and animals. In southern Appalachia, plants and animals that thrive in the northern part of the continent grow next to those that live in the southern part. The mountains and valleys of the region also create many biological pocket areas at different altitudes where still more variety is possible. Early people hunting and gathering in this region found not only a wealth of food but a tremendous choice, from elk to quail, from papaws to ginseng roots. In addition, the ground itself offered riches. Many rivers cut through this mountain region, creating valleys of great fertility. One of the earliest European settlers in the territory, a Moravian missionary, spoke of growing corn in the same field for thirty years. The corn grew abundantly year after year, even without fertilizing. The Cherokee built villages in the river valleys and farmed, hunted, and gathered there.

The earth and rocks of the mountains also provided people who lived there with clay for potting, hard stones for tool making, and silver and quartz. Quartz crystals, thought to be deep mirrors of the future, were treasured.

Cherokee culture took form through these resources. It also took root in the very shape of the landscape. To the Cherokee, mountain peaks were landmarks as familiar as the local city skyline is to modern Americans. Meadows and rivers were

locators too, letting Cherokee tribespeople know where they were as certainly as drivers today navigate with respect to a certain restaurant or a highway interchange.

Beyond location, though, the landscape held meaning in Cherokee beliefs and myths. A familiar meadow in the woods, for example, was known as the place where the Bear clan once held an important council. The scarring of the Cherokee River valley was thought to be caused by the gaming wheel of a mythic giant from ancient times. Even after the removal of most Cherokee to Oklahoma in the 1830s and the passing of several generations, Cherokee prayers and rituals still refer to the landscape of the Appalachian Mountains. A ritual call for relief from pain, for example, asks four ravens to bury the pain deep in a crevice

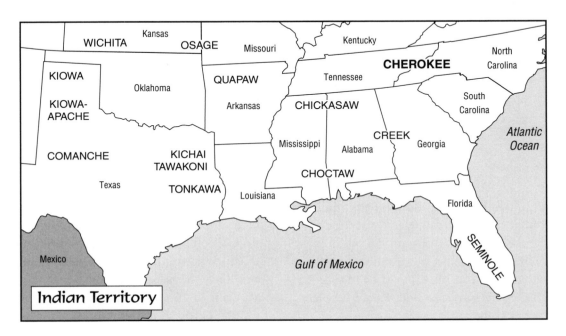

The Principal People

The Cherokee share many customs with other tribes in the southeast, including the Chickasaw, the Creek, and the Choctaw. Unlike their stocky neighbors, though, the Cherokee are a tall people, many over six feet. And they speak a language of the Iroquois type with origins in the northern part of the continent. The language and some very old Cherokee stories suggest that the Cherokee may have come to their land from somewhere north of the Ohio River. Ancient pottery and other evidence show the Cherokee were in their territory centuries before Columbus sailed for America, so any such migration must have taken place well over five hundred years ago.

The name "Cherokee" seems to have been given to the tribe by its neighbors. The word may come from a Muskogean term which means "people of a different speech." Or it may come from the Choctaw word for "cave people" (there are many caves in the mountains). Like many other Native Americans, the Cherokee refer to themselves simply as "the real people," or "the principal people." In Cherokee, that is *Ani-Yunwiya*.

Historians think there may have been about thirty thousand Cherokee in the Appalachians in 1650. Population figures for the years before European contact can be

A Cherokee hunter uses a blowgun to bring down small prey.

in Sanigilagi, the Cherokee name of a certain Appalachian peak: "Ha! You have put the Intruder [the pain] into a crevice of Sanigilagi that it may never find the way back. You have put it to rest in the Darkening Land, so that it may never return. Let the relief come."[3]

no more than rough estimates, but it is known that the Cherokee lived along rivers, in villages. A village usually included dwelling houses, a large council house (sometimes set on an earth mound), a flattened ceremonial ground, and a field used for ball play. Around each village were its farm fields. A web of trails connected the villages, gave access to the woods for hunting and gathering, and connected Cherokee lands with distant people and places for visiting, trading, or making war.

A Sense of Home

Any young person growing up in a traditional Cherokee village had a strong sense of home and family. Children were raised in houses that usually included plenty of relatives and several generations. The Cherokee traditionally trace families matrilineally, or through the mother's side of the family line. A typical household included a grandmother and her husband, any unmarried daughters and sons, and all married daughters with their husbands and children. Children grew up with cousins to play with as well as brothers and sisters, and with many relatives who helped support each other. Marriage itself was a simple agreement to live together. Some men took more than one wife; those who did often married a set of sisters. Marriage partners could leave one another for any reason, but the children as well as any household property not specifically tied to the husband remained with the wife and her family. Although separation was easy, many couples remained together for long periods or for life.

A family home was made up of a group of buildings: a roomy square or rectangular house, a round winter house, and several

How the Mountains Were Made

A Cherokee myth explains how the mountains of their homeland were created with the help of a great bird. This version, which is told today by Eastern Band storyteller Kathi Smith Littlejohn, is found in *Living Stories of the Cherokee,* edited by Barbara R. Duncan. It begins when the earth was very new, and still wet and muddy.

"And the buzzard flew off the rock with his great wings, and said, 'With the air from my wings, I'll make a fan and dry it so we can walk on this new land.' But each time when his wings went down, it would make a big valley, and each time the wings would go up, it would make a big mountain. And pretty soon the animals said, 'If we don't stop him there's not gonna be any land flat enough to walk on.' So they called him back, and today, when you look all around us, what do you see here? Mountains where his wings went up and made the mountains, and valleys where they went down. But if they hadn't stopped him, the whole world would look just like Cherokee."

Kana'ti and Selu

The story of Kana'ti and Selu is a traditional Cherokee myth that helps explain the need for men to hunt and for women to grow corn. This summary of the very long story is based on an account in *Myths of the Cherokee,* by James K. Mooney.

Among the first people on earth were a man and a woman, Kana'ti and Selu. (In Cherokee, *kana'ti* means "hunter" and *selu* means "corn.") Every day, Kana'ti brought home a game animal for meat, while Selu contributed corn for dinner. But no one knew how they got the food. The couple had a son who found a friend called Wild Boy. The two boys decided to find out where the food came from. They followed Kana'ti to the woods, keeping out of sight. To their surprise, they discovered that Kana'ti kept all the game animals hidden in a hole in the ground. They watched as Kana'ti let one out, shot it with his bow and arrow, and brought it home. The next day, the boys went to the woods to try to get an animal for themselves. By mistake, they let all the animals out. Now, people must go hunting all over the woods if they want meat.

The boys next tried to discover where Selu got the corn. They hid and watched her enter the storehouse. Once inside, she simply rubbed her body, and her basket filled with corn. The boys decided she was a witch and should be killed. Selu knew their thoughts and gave them instructions. Once she was dead, she said, they should clear land and drag her body around it seven times, then wait up all night. The boys agreed, killed her, and then followed *some* of her instructions. As a result, Selu's death allowed corn to grow from the earth, but because the boys did not obey all the corn woman's instructions, people must work hard at farming and wait for harvest.

After many adventures and many years, the boys arrived in the Upper World, above the arch of the sky. There they found Kana'ti and Selu sitting together in peace.

outbuildings. The houses were based on poles sunk into the ground, sided with interwoven mats, and roofed with bark. The walls were plastered with mud and clay. Deerskins covered doorways.

The family lived in the rectangular house most of the year. Inside, it was partitioned as needed for family members. Several fireplaces were set under roof openings which let the smoke out. During the coldest part of the winter, the family would move to its small, round winter house, where a low fire was kept burning continually. Having many people in a small space also helped keep the winter house warm.

Any woman in the family who was menstruating moved into a special small house during her periods. Food was brought to her there. To the Cherokee, menstruation meant a change in the habitual course of nature, a time when unusual or dangerous things might happen. It was safer to keep the women separate from the rest of the family during that time. Women also used these small houses for giving birth. Births were normally attended by a few women related to the mother, including a midwife. The baby's father and a priest were also often present, though they stood so that they did not view the birth directly.

Family houses were used and repaired as needed year after year. When a house became crowded, a man could build a new home for his wife and children. Usually, it was close to the houses of the wife's mother and sisters.

The Seven Clans

The idea of family extended even beyond housing compounds to include all the relatives of a person's mother: the clan. There may have been many clans in ancient times, but historically every Cherokee belonged to one of just seven clans. Each clan had a name which tied it to the real and mythic landscape of the Cherokee: Wolf, Bird, Deer, Long Hair, Wild Potato, Twister, and Blue. Each clan had stories and traditions which were passed on to the young by older members.

The clans had many functions in Cherokee life, but most importantly they gave each member a sense of identity and belonging. A child orphaned by illness or disaster would be adopted by the nearest eligible clan members. Any traveling Cherokee could be sure of a welcome at a household of his clan in any Cherokee village. The visitor would use family names for his hosts, calling everyone of his age "Brother" or "Sister," and calling people of his parents' or grandparents' generation "Mother" or "Father," "Grandmother" or "Grandfather." Because clans were considered to be families, both men and women had to marry outside the clan of their birth. But ties to a Cherokee's own clan, his or her mother's people, remained strong and meaningful for life.

Getting Corn and Meat

Most of the tasks of life among the traditional Cherokee were divided according to sex. The Cherokee tell a funny story about the different work of boys and girls:

The little Wren is the messenger of the birds, and she pries into everything. She gets up early in the morning and goes around to every house in the settlement to get news for the bird council. When a baby is born, she finds out whether it is a boy or girl and reports to the council. If it is a boy, she sings in mournful chorus, "Alas! The whistle of the arrow! My shins will burn," because the birds know when the boy grows older, he will hunt them with his blowgun and arrows and roast them on a stick.

But if the baby is a girl, the birds are glad and sing. "Thanks! The sound of the pestle! At her home I shall

Cherokee men and boys hunted birds with bows and arrows.

surely be able to scratch where she sweeps," because they know that after a while, they will be able to pick up stray grains where she beats the corn into meal.[4]

Men were responsible for hunting, and women for growing corn. The importance of these tasks was emphasized even at the Cherokee wedding ceremony, where the bride offered the groom ears of corn, while he offered her venison, the meat of the deer, which was the Cherokee's chief game animal. Men also made war while women raised children. This balance of duties for men and women was very important to the Cherokee, although in special circumstances people did step outside the customary roles: Women helped with some tasks of the hunt, for instance, and a few women even took part in battle. Women were certainly responsible for growing the crops, but men helped with field preparation and on certain planting and harvest days.

Planting, Gathering, and Preparing Food

Each family had its own field on the outskirts of the village. The size of the field depended on the number of people who needed to be fed and the number of women available to tend the growing crops. In addition, most women kept small kitchen gardens near their homes where they grew a kind of quick-growing corn and vegetables.

At times of planting and harvest in the large fields, everyone who was able to work would join together in each field by turn. An eighteenth-century visitor described the process in the spring:

> About an hour before sunrise, they enter the field agreed on by lot, and fall to work with great cheerfulness; sometimes one of their orators cheers them with jests and humorous old tales, and sings several of their most agreeable wild tunes, beating also with a stick in his right hand, on top of an earthen pot covered with a wet and well-stretched deer-skin; thus they proceed from field to field, till their seed is sown.[5]

The Cherokee planted corn seeds in little hills. Beans and squash were planted between the hills along with gourds, pumpkins, and sunflowers. Once the planting was done, women were responsible for weeding and keeping pests out of the fields. The women were also responsible for gathering food from the woods, an enormous job that included gathering nuts, roots, stems, leaves, berries, and honey, and collecting maple sap for sugar making.

In the autumn, the large village fields were harvested by the whole village. Families contributed a certain amount of food to community storage sheds. The women stocked their own sheds and pits and processed the food. Most corn and beans were dried in the field so they could be kept through the winter. Dried beans were soaked, then boiled to eat. The dry corn kernels were separated from their inedible hulls by soaking in lye made from wood ashes.

Cherokee Corn Dishes

The Cherokee made an amazing variety of foods with corn. Hot and cold drinks and soups were based on finely ground cornmeal mixed with water. One popular cold drink was a cornmeal broth which was allowed to sour, though not to become alcoholic. Cooks enriched cornmeal soup with various ingredients such as green grapes, honey locust pods, and nuts. Fresh corn was boiled briefly, then roasted over coals to eat. Sometimes corn prepared that way was added to stews of venison or other meat. Dry toasted or "parched" corn kernels were standard food for travelers and warriors.

Bread was the most popular way to eat corn. The basic bread dough was simply corn meal mixed with enough water to make a thick dough. Breads could take the form of dumplings or larger boiled doughs. Often bread was covered with a pot or wrapped in leaves, then set on a flat hearth rock with coals heaped over it to bake. Most often, Cherokee women baked their bread with added ingredients. Chestnuts and other nuts, called chinquapins, were very popular, as were black walnuts and hickory nuts. Beans were often added to the bread, making it higher in protein. Herbs, such as wild onion and sassafras, and smoke were sometimes used to flavor the bread. Most often, bread was served with a dip of bear grease or nut oil.

Europeans later imitated this process to make the dishes called "hominy" (originally a Native American word) and ground hominy "grits." Cherokee women ground up the dried, hulled corn to make flour. For this, they used a log set on end and partly hollowed out. The corn was placed in the hollow, then pounded with a long, heavy wood pestle that fit into the hollow. The flour was used to make a wide variety of breads.

In traditional villages, it was rare for people to be hungry. The many storage sheds provided food in emergencies. Families kept extra food for visitors, feasts, and to help needy clan members. Community food served ambassadors, traders, and even whole neighboring villages when disaster struck.

Making Useful Items

The division between men's and women's work extended to making the tools and implements needed for each job. Men made the equipment they needed for hunting, fishing, making war, and smoking. This included bows and arrows, hatchets and knives of stone, blowguns (long, hollow reeds through which darts were blown), fishnets, and pipes. Pipes were often elaborately carved from soapstone in the shape of animals and birds. The men did most of their hunting in the fall. The Cherokee roasted meat over a fire, or smoked and dried it for later use.

Women were responsible for making so many items of daily use that one early visitor called them "the chief manufacturers"[6] of the tribe. They dug local clay to make pottery, which they glazed over a fire to a shiny black finish. They made baskets to hold every kind of item, wove rugs from hemp or reeds, and made clothing from deerskins and fabrics woven from buffalo hair, hemp, or mulberry bark. One unusual

A Cherokee woman uses a mortar and pestle to grind corn.

piece of clothing made by the Cherokee was the feather cloak, a cape in which feathers were so densely interwoven that it looked like the back of a bird.

Standard clothing for Cherokee men was a breechcloth of deerskin. This garment was about a foot wide and several feet long. It went between the legs and draped over a belt in front and back. Cherokee men in the 1700s are also described as wearing a sewn, short breechcloth similar in shape to a modern racer's swimsuit. Women wore simple skin or fabric knee length skirts, with no top except for a necklace. Everyone wore moccasins. Children often went without clothes in warm weather. In winter, people wrapped skins and furs around themselves for warmth. Some clothing was elaborately decorated with beads or shells; women made necklaces, earrings, and other jewelry for both sexes. One Cherokee custom was to split the earlobes, stretch them, and wrap them in tooled silver. Men and women alike were tattooed over much of their bodies; paint was added for ceremonial occasions.

Medicine from "Each Tree, Shrub, Herb, Grass, and Moss"

A varied diet helped the Cherokee stay healthy, and so did their knowledge of many kinds of plants and herbs which they used as medicines. One Cherokee myth explains the "goodwill" of the plant world.

Traditional weapons and utensils made from bone, animal hide, and plant materials.

The story says that the deer first thought of giving man a disease because man hunted. Soon other animals chimed in, dreaming up new diseases. However, the plant world answered back. According to one storyteller, "Now when the friendly plants heard what the animals had decided, they decided to help the people. Each tree, shrub, herb, grass, and moss agreed to furnish a cure for one of the diseases named by the animals and insects."[7]

The Cherokee did not rely on plants alone to cure disease and heal injury. They thought that disease and injury were caused by an imbalance in the world due to someone's improper behavior. Therefore the plant remedies were usually accompanied by actions or words meant to restore balance. For example, a man with rheumatism might feel the troubling symptoms were caused by his failure to thank the spirit of a deer he recently hunted. To set this to rights, he could put a healing paste of herbs on his body while speaking (or asking a priest to speak) ritual words of thanks to the deer. The special words of thanks are one of many Cherokee "sacred formulas." These are ritual sayings, chants, songs, and prayers used for varied purposes. For centuries, the sacred words were memorized and passed down from generation to generation. In the 1800s, people began to write them down. The sacred formulas were part of the spiritual life of the Cherokee, which to them was inseparable from daily life. The things of their world, the cycle of nature and human activity in the mountains, made sense only as part of their worldview and system of belief.

Chapter 2

Belief and Community

When a Cherokee hunter gave thanks to the spirit of a deer he had just killed, or when a priest spoke ritual words to cure an illness, they were fitting in with a system of beliefs shared by all the Cherokee people. This system was a set of ideas and stories that explained the true state of things in the Cherokee view. It was a little like religion, science, and history rolled into one. While family ties united the Cherokee into several clans, the belief system united them all as one people.

The Upper World, the Under World, and the Ball of Mud

According to traditional Cherokee belief, the universe consisted of three "worlds." The physical world people know and live in lay in the middle. The sky was really the underside of a huge stone dome or sky vault. Above the vault was the Upper World, where immortal beings with special powers lived. These beings included the Sun, an ancient woman; her brother the Moon; and Thunder, among others.

The Sun was the most powerful force in the universe. Because the Sun measures out the days and the year, the Cherokee called her "the apportioner." The Sun, and to a lesser degree the Moon, represented predictability and the right order of things.

Long ago, according to Cherokee myth, all the animals and people were also living in the Upper World because there was no land below, only water. The story of the creation of our world is still being recounted by Cherokee and other Native Americans. Cherokee storyteller Mark Ball of Kentucky tells the tale this way:

> In the beginning, all human beings and animals lived above the sky vault. The beaver's grandchild, the water beetle, decided he would go and explore. He flew down and went all over the surface of the water, but he found no place to rest. So he dove down, and he brought up a ball of mud. This ball of mud began to grow and grow, until it became an island. This is what we call the earth today.[8]

☼ Going to Water

Priests were in charge of a variety of public ceremonies which brought the Cherokee community together. One of the most important of these, performed alone or with other rituals, is called "going to water." Going to water is a ritual of purification which involves bathing in the nearest running water. The Cherokee may have gone to water every morning in ancient times. Certainly they performed this ceremony often and for many reasons during the year. People went to water to prepare for ceremonial dances or for war, to halt disease or ensure health, to counteract bad dreams, or to mark the time of the new moon. Many ritual formulas and actions could be used to accompany going to water. Often, the priest called on the river itself, called "Long Person," for strength and renewal, as in this sacred formula, quoted by Alan Kilpatrick in *The Night Has a Naked Soul: Witchcraft and Sorcery Among the Western Cherokee:*

Long Person, you are in repose. Nothing can overpower you.

Now you are going to elevate my soul. You are going to renew it. Ha!

Now you have just come to elevate it. Long Person, I have just come bearing my soul.

Below this earth lay a mysterious Under World, a land where the Sun traveled at night on its way back from its setting place to its rising place. The ghosts or souls of the dead were thought to live there. In the Under World, many things were the opposite of what they are on earth, including the seasons. It was a land of monsters and ghosts and chaos, but also a place of fertility and creativity.

Keeping the Balance on Earth

Just as the Upper World and Under World had a balance point on earth, the Cherokee thought many forces and things had their opposites and had to be balanced. The four directions symbolized some of the opposites. East, the direction of sunrise, was associated with the color red and with birth. West, the direction of sunset, was connected with the color black and with death. North was the direction of cold, blue, and defeat, and South the direction of warmth, white, and peace. Similarly, male was thought of as the opposite of female, fire the opposite of water, plants the opposite of animals. As a consequence, misfortunes were often thought to be caused by one force overwhelming its opposite. It followed that to correct misfortunes, people had to take steps to restore the balance. Such restoration might range from holding a special ceremony to making war against neighbors who had attacked.

Balance could be maintained also by keeping forces apart from each other, each force in its proper category separate from its opposite. Thus fire was never doused with water. Instead, the Cherokee put their fires out with earth. Women were sepa-rated from men at times of the month when their female force was thought to be at its peak. Men preparing for war, when they were at their most masculine, were

Cherokee people perform the Beaver Dance, one of many dances that reflect ancient beliefs.

Powerful Spirits, Mighty Women

Various spirit beings were thought to live in the Upper and Under Worlds, and sometimes they came out to influence human beings. The most powerful creature of the Under World was the Uktena, an enormous snake with horns, wings, and four legs. On its forehead the Uktena bore a stone crystal which could be used to foretell the future. Quartz crystals used by the Cherokee for that purpose were said to be related to the Uktena's crystal.

Unusual people were honored just as unusual spirits were. A small number of women gained the title of "War Woman." A War Woman was someone who proved her valor by an unusual deed of war. It was not enough to accompany a war party as a cook or helper. One War Woman gained her status by inventing a clever battle strategy. Others gained it by actually killing enemies. War Women had ceremonial and council rights generally reserved for experienced warriors, and they were in charge of deciding prisoners' fates.

arate, seemed to be confused. For example, evergreen plants such as cedar and laurel seemed to live on through winter, unlike most plants. The evergreens were used often as physical and spiritual medicines because of their apparently special powers. Frogs and turtles had four feet and walked on earth like other animals, but they also spent much time under water. To the Cherokee, such animals stood out. They might give people unusual help, such as guiding a person through the Under World, or do people unusual harm.

Witches and Priests

The ordered world of the Cherokee was threatened by all kinds of imbalances, but some of the greatest threats seemed to come from creatures who looked just like ordinary people. Such a creature, in human shape but full of disguised ill will and armed with special powers, was given a name translated into English as "witch." Witches could easily change shape. Though they might look like people, they were inhuman, pitiless, and preyed on the community. A variation on the witch idea was the stone-covered, invulnerable spirit called Spearfinger. Disguised as an old woman, Spearfinger could kill people simply by poking them with her finger. Another witchlike creature was the Raven Mocker, a kind of being which, according to old accounts collected by James Mooney in the 1890s, "flies through the air in fiery shape, with arms outstretched like wings, and sparks trailing behind. . . . Every little while as he flies he makes a

also required to keep separate from women for several days before a raid.

The Cherokee paid special attention to cases where opposites seemed to be mixed, or where categories, normally sep-

cry like the cry of a raven."[9] Raven Mockers were believed to have the power to remove human hearts without appearing to touch their victims.

The Cherokee believed in witches for the same reasons other peoples have around the world at various times in history. They lived in a small society bound by powerful social rules. When something went wrong in this kind of society, people looked for a reason. It was easy to blame someone who appeared to be odd, such as a twin, a neighbor with a grudge, or a person who seemed to avoid company. A Cherokee anthropologist, Alan Kilpatrick, writes that "the Cherokee witch represents a supernatural force beyond social control."[10] When Cherokee tribespeople thought they had detected a witch, they had a right to kill the person immediately because the threat to the community was so great.

Often, though, ordinary people could not find the source of misfortune, or were not sure what to do about it. Then, they could call on a ritual specialist. In ancient times, that person would have been a kind of priest. Cherokee priests began to learn from older priests as children and went through years of training. They memorized hundreds of spoken formulas, songs and chants; learned many ceremonial actions; practiced finding and mixing herbs and other materials for curing and rituals; and learned the stories about the nature of this world, the Upper World, and the Under World. Priests were thought to have supernatural powers through their actions and words, although sometimes these powers were thwarted by circumstances or by stronger powers.

Priests, both male and (for certain purposes) female, took part in regular town ceremonies and meetings. They could also be called upon by families or clans to help counter suspected evil forces and to ensure good fortune. A major priestly activity was to help heal the sick and wounded, since all illness was thought to have its cause in some human, animal, or spirit action which created an imbalance or impurity. There were probably different sorts or ranks of priests. After the Cherokee came into contact with Europeans and the power of priests was reduced, the term "conjurer" or "medicine man" was generally used in English to name the person who filled the priest's role. The Cherokee word is *adonisgi*.

Ritual, Music, and Dance

The *adonisgi* directed ceremonies to mark important times of the year. One account tells of six major festivals, with minor ones at every new moon. Irregular ceremonies helped to kick off a hunt, a raid, or a ball game. Elements of these ceremonies lasted into the 1900s and are still performed, in reduced form, today.

Music and dance remain major parts of Cherokee ceremony. Some festivals consist mostly of dancing all night long. Drums, rattles, and voices provide the music. Traditional drums were ceramic pots with a deerskin stretched across the top. Rattles were made from gourds and often from turtle or terrapin shells filled with

Members of a tribe perform the Eagle Dance dressed in ceremonial Cherokee clothing.

pebbles. Women attached the turtle rattles to their legs so they could emphasize the rhythm of the dance. Traditional Cherokee singers use a four- or five-note scale, which produces melodies quite different from those based on the European seven-note scale. Cherokee ritual songs typically include seven phrases repeated four times.

The dances, some of which are still performed, have meaningful themes. Many are connected with specific clans. Some focus on the qualities of an animal. In the Bear Dance, for instance, the men circle the fire, stepping in time to a drum and growling like bears. Then the women enter and dance back and forth with the men. According to a Cherokee expert, "at one point in the dance the actors raise their heads and tear the air over their shoulders in imitation of the dance presumed to be performed by bears."[11]

The Green Corn Ceremony

In July or August, when the corn ripened enough to harvest, Cherokee women would start cleaning their homes and throwing out food from the previous year. Men would sweep out the council house, build temporary shelters at the public ground, whitewash buildings, and carry out ashes. It was time for the greatest festival of the year, the Green Corn Ceremony.

In ancient times, this grand ceremony was probably two: a harvest ceremony plus a ceremony of reconciliation, in which everyone forgave enemies and ended quarrels. Later, these two purposes were united in one. The theme of the Green Corn Ceremony was renewal of the crop, of relations in the community, and even of the sacred fire which represented the sun and was a symbol of all life.

When the village was in order, the warriors and elders, called "beloved men" and "beloved women," went to the ceremonial ground to begin a fast of two nights and a day. Sentinels protected them as the beloved women prepared a drink of sacred medicine. The drink worked as an emetic, and made the warriors who drank it vomit. This procedure was thought to purify their bodies. At the end of the fast, all fires in the village having been put out, a priest would light a new fire. On it he would place fresh corn brought to him by the women. Everyone seeking forgiveness could come forward, for every fault and crime except murder was forgiven at that time. Next, the women took coals from the new fire to light the fires in their own homes. When the women came back, feasting on the new corn began, followed by dancing and singing. The ceremony

Public Games and Ritual

The Cherokee played certain games that involved many community members. These games had ceremonial meaning, even though some of that meaning is unclear today. The game of chunkey was played on a long, narrow, cleared space. There two men at a time played, while others watched and bet on the outcome. To play, one man would roll the heavy disk-shaped chunkey stone along the ground. Then each man would throw a pole toward the spot where he thought the disc would stop. The closest pole won points. The game was good practice for spear throwing in war or in hunting. Native Americans all across the continent played this game, some with a hoop and spear instead of the stone disc and poles. The chunkey yard was also used for rituals and for parading or torturing prisoners.

At the center of the chunkey yard was a large pole used for the "single pole ball game." In this game, women played against men, vying for posession of a ball made of stuffed deerskin. The team that could hit the pole above a certain mark, or on its crowning object, gained points. In this game, the men held in each hand a stick that terminated in a small webbed basket. It was common for men to bet venison on the outcome of the game, while women bet corn, echoing the traditional balance of tasks between the sexes.

The full ball game, sometimes called "stickball," pitted teams of men from rival towns against each other on a large playing field. Each player used his pair of webbed sticks, which resembled lacrosse sticks, to throw and catch a ball. The goal was for each team to send the ball through a pair of poles at their opponents' end of the field, as in American football. The game was surrounded in ritual, including going to water for team members and use of a priest as a kind of cheerleader. Sometimes hundreds of men competed at once. Injuries and even deaths during the game were common.

ended when the people painted themselves with white clay, symbolizing peace, and went to water for ritual bathing.

In the House of the Sacred Fire

The work of priests, the *adonisgi,* was important in the general government of a Cherokee town. In the council house, religious and nonreligious activities were melded together. Law was a spiritual matter even more than a practical matter for the community. One clear sign of this was the major speech made by the high priest at the Green Corn Ceremony. Dressed in full regalia, he recited the laws and rules of the community, laws said to be kept by the sacred fire. The worst thing about breaking a law or rule was not the punishment or public ridicule that might follow. It was the fact that the sacred fire and the spirit world would know.

The community's sacred fire was tended in the round council house in winter and at the open ceremonial ground in summer. The council house was an enlarged version of the winter house. The ceremonial ground was probably a large version of the summer house, without the roof and some of the walls. These could be built by one large village or several settlements. The area served by a council house made up a "town" according to the first European observers. A more accurate name may be "chiefdom," a term that means a community with a recognized chief but with less political control over individuals than most modern governments.

Like other southeastern tribes, the Cherokee had two kinds of government: the White, or peacetime, government and the Red, or wartime, government. The governments were not in power at the same time. Chiefs were chosen by general consent of the people, elders and warriors having the strongest influence. During peacetime, the White chief (probably also a priest) worked with his council of representatives from each of the clans. In addition, certain "beloved old men" gave their advice, as did some "beloved old women." The Red government consisted of a Red or war chief and the most important warriors. "War Women" who had actually fought under extraordinary circumstances were included. The Red council was thus younger than the White, and was more flexible.

The tasks of the White council included meeting with visitors and ambassadors, deciding on building projects and repairs for the chiefdom, making arrangements for festivals and ceremonies, determining dates for general agricultural jobs, and dealing with other matters related to the well-being of the whole community. The Red council met to determine war strategy.

Although leaders were male, any man, woman, or child could get a hearing at a council meeting. In large meetings, people were seated in sections by clan, with men in front, then women, and then children behind. When the Cherokee leader Attakullakulla first visited a colonial South Carolina council meeting, he was astonished to see no women in the group. He pointed out to the governor that "White Men as well as Red were born of Women."[12]

The goal of any Cherokee meeting was to reach consensus, or unanimous agreement. The value placed on consensus was so great that the Cherokee were willing to debate an issue for days or even weeks to achieve it. A scholar writes about the human qualities most admired by the Cherokee under such circumstances: "A good man was a man who avoided conflict with his fellows. He asserted his own rights cautiously: he avoided situations which might entail conflict; and he withdrew from men who were contentious or disrespectful. Harmony was essential."[13]

To Make the Punishment Fit the Crime

The council of a Cherokee chiefdom had little to do with crime and punishment, which was considered to be a private matter between individuals or clans. The ruling principle of justice was the Cherokee's central spiritual idea of balance. A wrongful act required an equal act against it. At the simplest level, a child who was struck by another with a stick was expected to strike that person back with a stick. A different kind of counter at-

tack, such as throwing a stone or tripping the person, would be considered inappropriate. The person who had wronged another was expected to take his punishment quietly.

Justice in the Cherokee tribe was based on the idea of punishment fitting the crime.

Council Houses and Ceremonial Grounds

Council houses were usually about twenty-five feet in diameter, although some were much larger. The council house at Chota, one of the oldest Cherokee towns, was said to hold five hundred people. All around the wall were ample benches or couches, in several tiers, for the people meeting in council, with seven sections set aside by clan. In later years, the national Cherokee council house was built as a septagon (with seven sides). The couches in council houses also served as beds for visitors or community members who for some reason needed a place to sleep away from home. At the center of the council house, the firewood was often arranged in a circle or spiral. The sacred fire made its way around the ring, brightening the otherwise dark building. At the ceremonial ground, fire was also a focal point, while people were ranged on benches beneath arbors all around. The four sides of the ceremonial ground were laid out along the four directions, with the chief's benches on the west side facing east.

What made this kind of justice practical was the presence of the community. Everyone knew everyone else and watched what was going on. Retaliation did not often continue past one response because family and neighbors would not allow it. In fact, most minor problems were corrected by means of public disapproval or ridicule. Boastful people were subject to catcalls, whistles, and laughter at council meetings. People who avoided their chores were likely to be insulted and talked about.

The one unforgivable crime to the Cherokee was killing another Cherokee. Like other crimes, it called for equal retaliation. Since the dead victim could not undertake this task, the victim's clan members—especially older brothers—were expected to do it. If the murderer ran away or hid, the avenging clan was expected to kill a member of the murderer's clan instead. In some cases, this system led to rapid justice. However, the Cherokee system did not allow for fact-finding or explanations on the part of the accused. A death caused by a human action had to be avenged, even if the death was accidental. Witch killings were particularly divisive because people did not always agree about who was a witch and who was not. In one case, a witch killing led to an interclan feud that resulted in the revenge killings of seven people.

War

Warfare was a continual part of Cherokee life, but it consisted mainly of groups of warriors going on raids against other tribes. The raids were usually a response to earlier attacks or actions which the warriors thought merited retaliation. In fact, war was considered the most elaborate and heroic form of justice, or restoring the balance of the universe.

War-making often began with a few men beating drums in the village to assemble other men willing to go on a raid. If enough could be assembled, they would select a Red war chief, who would displace the White chief. In council, the warriors would decide when and how to attack. They would next prepare for war with days of fasting and performing such purification rituals as going to water.

Village dance and ceremony sent the warriors on their way, and the raid itself was surrounded by religious rituals and rules of behavior. It was important to feel that the invisible forces of the universe were on their side. A well-known legend told of spirits who would come in the form of Cherokee warriors to help the people when they were in the most extreme danger. These spirits were said to have emerged from the ancient mound at the Cherokee town of Nikwasi to help defeat the Creek tribes. In the words of a modern Cherokee storyteller,

> they kill all of the Creeks except for one,
>
> And he goes back and tells all the Creek brothers and sisters,
>
> "Never mess with the village of Nikwasi,

because they have spirit people who protect it."[14]

Although some warfare was prolonged, most raids were quick. Warriors grabbed a few prisoners and killed a few of the enemy, taking their scalps if possible and some possessions as trophies. A scalp was the person's hair and the skin, with some flesh, to which it was attached. On the return of the war party, the village celebrated. Scalps were tied to poles in the chunkey yard, the gaming field near the council house. Warriors retold their deeds and gained the credit they needed for social standing. Then, they retired for ritual cleansing and left the prisoners to the women.

The women often tortured the prisoners in retaliation for the pain they thought had been inflicted on their own warriors. Beating, burning, and piercing were common methods of torture. Some prisoners were killed. Some were kept as slaves, though mainly they were trophies for their owners. Others, however, might be adopted by village families. Adoption of a prisoner appealed to the Cherokee because it was a way to replace a valuable family member who might have been lost. It made sense as a way to restore balance.

Chapter 3

The "Civilization" of the Cherokee

In the spring of 1540, members of the Spanish expedition of Hernando de Soto trudged into Cherokee territory. The Cherokee were probably not surprised to see these oddly dressed men in shining metal hats, riding animals that looked like heavy, hornless deer—they would have heard of the white men's progress from other tribes. Though short on corn, perhaps because of the season, the Cherokee politely offered seven hundred turkeys. Their guests ate, rested, then departed westward, as their chronicler, a nobleman from the Portuguese city of Elvas, wrote, "over very rough and lofty ridges."[15] This first encounter between Cherokee and Europeans was a quiet one, but it proved to be the beginning of enormous changes in Cherokee life brought about by the coming of Europeans and their culture to North America.

The Great Dying

The earliest change caused by Europeans resulted from disease microbes. Native Americans were especially susceptible to European diseases because they had never been exposed to them and so had not developed any natural resistance or immunity. Of perhaps thirty-two to thirty-five thousand Cherokee living in 1685, only about sixteen thousand remained by 1700. Even after that, epidemics of smallpox continued to ravage their settlements.

The loss of so many people was bound to leave holes in the cultural fabric of Cherokee life. Many of the dead were elders whose knowledge could not then be passed on, while others were valuable hunters, farmers, and clan leaders. Worst of all, the Cherokee were horrified when their priests were unable to cure diseases or save lives. The natural conclusion from their way of thinking was that they had brought disease on themselves by violating rules of purity and balance. Many Cherokee, according to a European witness, killed themselves out of shame when infected with smallpox: "some shot themselves, others cut their throats, some

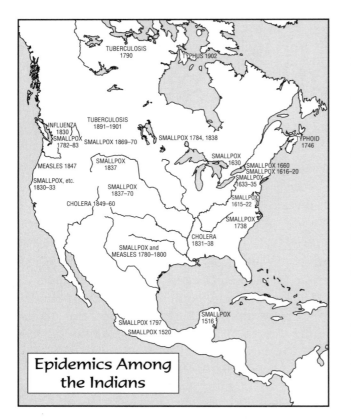

TUBERCULOSIS
1790

TYPHUS 1902

INFLUENZA
1830
SMALLPOX
1782–83 SMALLPOX 1869–70

TUBERCULOSIS
1891–1901

SMALLPOX 1784, 1838

TYPHOID
1746

MEASLES 1847

SMALLPOX
1837

SMALLPOX
1630 SMALLPOX 1660
SMALLPOX 1616–20
SMALLPOX
1633–35

SMALLPOX, etc.
1830–33

SMALLPOX
1837–70

SMALLPOX
1615–22

CHOLERA 1849–60

SMALLPOX
1738

CHOLERA
1831–38

SMALLPOX and
MEASLES 1780–1800

SMALLPOX 1797
SMALLPOX 1520

SMALLPOX
1516

**Epidemics Among
the Indians**

the coast to Cherokee towns for the purpose of exchanging guns for deerskins. Deerskins brought a good price in the English colonies.

In 1700, most Cherokee were living in sixty to seventy towns in four geographic areas: the northerly Middle Towns and Overhill Towns in present-day North Carolina and Tennessee, and the Lower Towns and Valley Towns in present-day South Carolina and Georgia. Divided by mountain ridges, the people of each district spoke a somewhat different dialect of Cherokee. To organize the trade, a few Englishmen came to live among the people. They stored goods in their houses, made exchanges with Cherokee individuals, and took periodic trips to the cities along the coast to buy and sell.

Most of the resident traders took Cherokee wives, a practice which helped them learn the language and gain connections. Their children naturally became Cherokee clan members because the mothers were Cherokee. The fact that the Cherokee fully accepted these and many later intermarriages meant that the tribe quickly came to include a large percentage of "mixed-blood" people.

One of the first changes brought about by trade was in the way the Cherokee dressed. The trader's cloth was easy to sew and did not have to be first hunted or

stabbed themselves . . . many threw themselves with sudden madness into the fire, and there slowly expired, as if they had been utterly divested of the native power of feeling pain."[16]

Deerskins for Guns and Goods

In spite of disease and loss, the Cherokee were curious about Europeans and eager to trade with them. The most valuable European item by far was the gun, which changed forever the Cherokee's ways of hunting and making war. By 1700, English traders had established clear paths from

processed. The Cherokee soon were making clothing out of it, including the men's turban, fashionable in Europe at the time. Women began to cover themselves with more than a skirt when they found that Europeans thought it necessary.

The Cherokee were delighted with trade goods for other purposes, too. Iron pots lasted longer than ceramic ones and came ready-made. Metal hoes made the women's farming easier. Above all, the gun and ammunition allowed the men to kill more game and gain ever more trade goods.

However, the "improvements" brought by trade undermined many aspects of traditional Cherokee life. Hunting, which produced marketable skins, became more prestigious than farming. The old balance between the contributions of men and of women to the life of the tribe was thrown off. And, as people began to think of game as a product to be sold, the spiritual practices surrounding hunting were abandoned. Deer, wrote one observer, "were killed for their skins alone; and frequently the bodies were left to be devoured by the beasts and birds of prey."[17] As early as 1725, this new

Indians trade deerskins to Europeans for guns, the weapon that revolutionized the way Natives hunted and fought.

The Booger Dance

A new kind of dance appeared on Cherokee dance grounds after the arrival of Europeans. The Booger dancers, all men, wear strangely contorted wood masks with long noses. They burst in on the assembled people by surprise, making rude noises. They tease the girls and grab at them. Then they dance around the fire, but seem to get the dance steps all wrong. They shout crude remarks and stumble over people. Finally they leave as suddenly as they came. The Booger Dance seems to be a parody of European behavior. It is partly funny, and partly scary. Booger Dance masks made over many generations have shown great inventiveness, and the dance shows that Cherokee traditions are still evolving.

way of living was so well planted that one Cherokee chief told a British trade commissioner that "they [the Cherokee] must consider that they could not live without the English."[18]

War and More War

Like hunting, making war became increasingly important to the Cherokee after European contact. Guns made war easier in a way, and certainly more deadly. Neighboring tribes, pushed from their lands by European settlements, came into more conflict with one another. The Cherokee were often the winners in these skirmishes because their mountain territory was farther from settlements and because they were allies of the English.

Another new reason for war was the sale of captives. Along with the Europeans had come the institution of slavery. Like other tribes, the Cherokee found that they could sell war prisoners to slaveholding colonists. Sometimes, in raids on settlements, they captured African slaves and then sold them elsewhere. Some white traders encouraged war raids so that Cherokee who were in debt could pay their bills. The practice never involved large numbers of people at a time, but it was enough to mix the cultures of enslaved Africans and Native Americans in South Carolina and elsewhere.

By far the greatest reason for increased war was the influence of European powers. The French and English competed for the trade and loyalty of Native American tribes, and used them in battle. As war became more frequent and more intense, Red chiefs and warriors gained more power in Cherokee towns. Aggressive young warriors made decisions without the counsel of the beloved old men or women.

The Cherokee remained fairly loyal to the British until 1760, when some Virginians attacked their warriors. The angry Cherokee switched to French allegiance, defeated a force of twelve hundred British regulars, and took over a British fort. In retaliation, the British sent an overwhelming force of twenty-six hundred to smash the Cherokee. Hundreds of Cherokee died in the attack and hundreds more were driven from their burning villages to starve in the woods.

By the time of the American Revolution, however, the Cherokee were back on the side of the British. This wave of warfare gave the greatest blow yet to the Cherokee way of life. James Mooney describes the tribe at the end of the war:

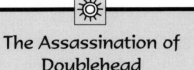

The Assassination of Doublehead

In 1806, Chief Doublehead and some others arranged for the sale of 10 million acres, the last great hunting ground of the Cherokee. Some of the money from the sale was to go not to the Cherokee treasury but to pay off personal debts owed to traders. When this story became public, many Cherokee were furious. One night before a ball play, Doublehead sat drinking in a tavern. Suddenly, the candle was blown out and unknown men shot the chief. He survived the shooting and was carried to a house, but there the assassins returned to finish their work. Doublehead died, and soon rumors spread the identity of the killers. Yet no relatives of Doublehead stepped forward to take revenge, probably because the killing was considered a kind of official punishment for the loss of the land.

More than fifty of their towns had been burned, their orchards cut down, their fields wasted, their cattle and horses killed or driven off, their stores of buckskin and other personal property plundered. Hundreds of their people had been killed or had died of starvation and exposure, others were prisoners in the hands of the Americans, and some had been sold into slavery. Those who had escaped were fugitives in the mountains, living upon acorns, chestnuts, and wild game, or were refugees with the British. From the Virginia line to the Chattahoochee the chain of destruction was complete. For the present at least any further resistance was hopeless, and they were compelled to sue for peace.[19]

A Farm with a Warm House on It

The Treaty of Hopewell, which brought peace between the United States and the Cherokee, said the United States alone could make agreements with the tribe. Soon the government provided a federal agent and a federal trade representative or "factor" to regulate trade between the Cherokee and others. A council of Cherokee chiefs was supposed to work with the agent, although many towns were in disarray. Only two divisions of towns existed by 1783: the Upper Towns and the Lower Towns.

The goal of American policy toward the Cherokee and other Indians was to lead them to become just like their European American neighbors. Thomas Jefferson explained this in 1808:

> Let me entreat you, therefore, on lands now given you to begin to give every man a farm; let him enclose it, cultivate it, build a warm house on it, and when he dies, let it belong to his wife and children after him. Nothing is so easy as to learn to cultivate the earth; all your women understand it. . . . If the men will take the labor of the earth from the women, they will learn to spin and weave and to clothe their families. . . . When once you have property, you will want laws and magistrates to protect your property and person. . . . You will find our laws are good for this purpose.[20]

"Civilization" in Jefferson's opinion depended on private property. Instead of holding land in common, he wanted the people to establish their own farms and act out of self-interest. A benefit of this idea to Jefferson and others was that once the Cherokee were farmers, hunting grounds would become unnecessary. They could be taken and divided among land-hungry Americans.

The Cherokee were not generally happy with the government program. Some gladly accepted free plows, metal hoes, and spinning wheels passed out by the federal agent. But farming got a slow start. Men had been raised to think of warfare and hunting as the activities that defined them as men. Now there was no warfare, and hunting had become difficult in the reduced grounds that remained.

The creation of private farms headed by men cut into basic Cherokee traditions in other ways. Women had always been the chief farmers. Men were hesitant to take on their role, even though it would free the women to spin and weave. Besides, the Cherokee were not used to European customs such as fencing pastures and fertilizing or rotating crops. Finally, building family houses on farms helped diminish the villages. War had already caused some people to move away from villages since they had been such easy targets. As the village disappeared or lost importance, so did the common social and religious life surrounding the council house.

The "Whole Cherokee Nation" Gains a Voice

As Cherokees moved slowly toward individual farming, their land was disappearing before their eyes. Over half of traditional Cherokee lands had been taken away between 1700 and the end of the Revolutionary War by settlers, colonies, and the new federal government. After the war, though, the losses continued. The federal agent kept arranging for the sale of parcels to various states. In a narrow legal sense, these sales bore the approval of the Cherokee. But in fact, only a minority of Lower Towns chiefs living near the agency had given their approval. Return J. Meigs, the agent after 1802, was not interested in the opinion of less friendly, more distant chiefs.

The Five Civilized Tribes

During the 1820s, other tribes in the Southeast were changing, like the Cherokee toward ways of living more like those of their white neighbors. The tribes of the Chickasaw, Choctaw, Creek and later the Seminole were grouped together with the Cherokee by public opinion as the "five civilized tribes." The condescending name suggested that the tribes had become tamely civilized through contact with whites and that other Indians were not civilized. However, the name did sound positive to most Americans at the time, and it brought the Cherokee good publicity as they fought to keep their land and rights. The name has actually lasted to the present day because the tribes ended up together in the western Indian Territory. Today they sometimes refer to themselves as the "Five Tribes" and cooperate in many ways.

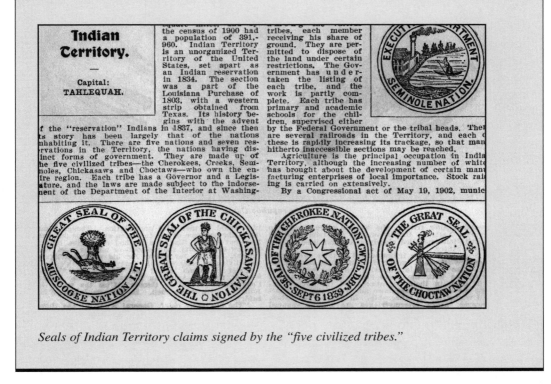

Indian Territory.

—

Capital:
TAHLEQUAH.

the census of 1900 had a population of 391,960. Indian Territory is an unorganized Territory of the United States, set apart as an Indian reservation in 1834. The section was a part of the Louisiana Purchase of 1803, with a western strip obtained from Texas. Its history begins with the advent f the "reservation" Indians in 1837, and since then ts story has been largely that of the nations nhabiting it. There are five nations and seven reservations in the Territory, the nations having disinct forms of government. They are made up of he five civilized tribes—the Cherokees, Creeks, Seminoles, Chickasaws and Choctaws—who own the enire region. Each tribe has a Governor and a Legislature, and the laws are made subject to the indorsement of the Department of the Interior at Washington.

tribes, each member receiving his share of ground. They are permitted to dispose of the land under certain restrictions. The Government has undertaken the listing of each tribe, and the work is partly complete. Each tribe has primary and academic schools for the children, supervised either by the Federal Government or the tribal heads. Ther are several railroads in the Territory, and each o these is rapidly increasing its trackage, so that man hitherto inaccessible sections may be reached.

Agriculture is the principal occupation in Indian Territory, although the increasing number of white has brought about the development of certain man facturing enterprises of local importance. Stock rai ing is carried on extensively.

By a Congressional act of May 19, 1902, munic

Seals of Indian Territory claims signed by the "five civilized tribes."

Within a few years, chiefs in the Lower Towns near the agency began talking with Meigs about exchanging their land for new land in the Arkansas territory. A delegation of chiefs left for Washington to settle the matter. Then Upper Towns Cherokee found out what had happened and sent their own delegates to object. The affair ended with some loss of land and some people departing for Arkansas. But it also led to a gathering of chiefs from all over the Cherokee territory in 1809. They decided to unite, to have regular meetings, and to name a standing National Committee of thirteen men to carry out the business of the tribe.

Outsiders such as the federal agent would no longer have such an influence over Cherokee self-government, or take advantage of divisions among the people. "It has now been a long time that we have been much confused and divided in our opinions," the council wrote to agent Meigs, "but now we have settled our affairs to the satisfaction of both parties and become as

Meeting between General Andrew Jackson, who favored the removal of the Natives, and Cherokee warrior Weatherford.

one. You will now hear from us not from the lower towns nor the upper towns but from the whole Cherokee Nation."[21]

The tribal unity of 1809 did not bring an end to political or cultural struggles. A period of unease began in 1811 when some Cherokees called for a return to the old beliefs and ways of the tribe. This movement was strengthened when great earthquakes shook the ground. Unlike some tribal movements of this kind, the Cherokee revival did not call for retribution against white people. The emphasis was on renewing old values which had certainly been eroded by European-American culture. In some towns, dancing went on for days and the people went to water as they had not done in years.

The movement ended when the Cherokee Nation went to war once again. Their neighbors, a group of Creek called the Red Sticks, were threatening the United States along with other tribes west of the Appalachians. The Cherokee agreed to join American forces in fighting them. The Creek war went well for the Cherokee: Many young warriors distinguished themselves fighting proudly next to American soldiers. Their commander, General Andrew Jackson, praised their bravery. Yet just a few years after the end of the war, Jackson argued for the removal of all the Cherokee to the west. In a crisis in 1817 and 1818, the government threatened to put a treaty in place which would have required most Cherokee to exchange their homelands for western land, while others accepted "reserves" of farmland and be-

came citizens. The treaty failed to pass the Congress, though the idea remained alive. Meanwhile, a series of extraordinary developments seemed to promise a bright future.

The Cherokee "Renaissance"

During the 1820s, some Cherokee families, perhaps about three hundred, had achieved Jefferson's goal of profitable farming. The most prosperous Cherokee, a small minority, were slaveholding planters or mill owners, just like their neighbors in the southern states. They sent their children to schools that had been established by Moravian, Presbyterian, and Congregationalist missionaries.

A major event of the 1820s was the invention of a written form of the Cherokee language. A tribe member named Sequoyah developed symbols for each of the eighty-six syllables in his language. Authors of a textbook of beginning Cherokee tell what happened when the syllabary, or list of symbols, was given to the people:

> Cherokees took up writing with delight. Young braves would take trips for the pleasure of writing home. Family members left notes for one another around the house and taught one another the letters. In a few months the whole nation was reading and writing. It was a triumph.[22]

In a short time, the syllabary brought literacy and pride to every corner of the Cherokee lands. By 1825, people were beginning a written literature which joined the oral tradition of the past. In 1828, the

National Council provided for the first national newspaper, the *Cherokee Phoenix*. It featured articles in English and in the Cherokee syllabary, thanks to a special font of print designed for the purpose.

In the meantime, the National Council passed a series of eleven laws to establish a more workable government. This effort was completed in the formal written Cherokee Constitution of 1827, which mirrored that of the United States in many ways. Elias Boudinot, later editor of the tribe's newspaper, spoke in Philadelphia about the new government and the new Cherokee prosperity: "I can view my native country, rising from the ashes of her degradation, wearing her purified and beautiful garments, taking her seat with the nations of the earth."[23] The comeback since the Revolutionary War seemed to many people to be a real rebirth, a Cherokee "renaissance."

The Gathering Storm of Removal

After the passage of the Cherokee Constitution, the tribe seemed stronger than ever. Traditional Cherokee and those who had adopted European ways were brought together. A majority of the elected council followed traditional ways, but John Ross, a planter who was one-eighth Cherokee, was elected Principal Chief of the nation.

In 1828, Andrew Jackson was elected president of the United States. Jackson had long favored removal of the Cherokee and had helped send other tribes westward already. The states surrounding the Cherokee felt strongly that they had a right to the land. As one man reported, "Indeed, sir, there is only one point on which all Parties, both high and low, in

Sequoya, the author of the Cherokee written language.

Part of the front page of the Cherokee Phoenix *newspaper.*

Georgia agree, and that is that they all want the Indian Lands!"[24] The matter came to a boil when gold was discovered on Cherokee land. Georgians poured into the area to scramble for gold without regard for territorial borders. The state sent in armed men called the "Georgia Guard" to keep order; in fact, they defended intruders and arrested innocent Cherokee, including Principal Chief John Ross. Two years later, Jackson's party pushed the Indian Removal Bill through Congress. It called for the removal

of all Indian tribes in American territory westward across the Mississippi. Opponents of the bill protested in vain. "Do the obligations of justice change with the color of the skin?"[25] asked one outraged congressman. Three days after the Removal Bill was signed, Georgia sent 320 surveyors into Cherokee land to divide it into parcels to be given to Georgians by lottery.

The area claimed by Georgia included the Cherokee capital of New Echota and the homes and plantations of many tribe leaders, including John Ross. Quickly, leaders decided to move the government temporarily to Red Clay, in Tennessee.

Betrayal at New Echota

Leaders of the fight against the Removal Bill in Congress told Cherokee leaders, including young John Ridge, that there was no more they could do. At that point, Ridge decided that the best idea was to negotiate with the federal government for as much money and land in the west as possible in return for peacefully leaving the Cherokee homeland.

John Ridge was joined in his efforts by his cousin Elias Boudinot, and by his father, Major Ridge, also known as The Ridge. The Ridge was one of the most respected of the old Cherokee leaders. Made a major in the Creek war, he had long urged his people to stay and resist the whites who wanted them out. Now, Major Ridge began to travel around the Cherokee nation asking people to change their minds.

The great majority of Cherokee stood firm with Chief John Ross against leaving voluntarily, but a minority favored it. The nation debated the issue in a series of great council meetings. Rival groups of delegates went to Washington to work out terms. In the end, however, those who favored removal could not convince the others to agree.

At last the Removal minority arranged a council meeting in the former capital of New Echota in 1835. Ross and most other leaders stayed away to protest the removal idea. However, seventy-five people claiming to have the authority of the whole tribe signed a treaty with the federal government. The Treaty of New Echota gave away all the Cherokee lands in exchange for land in the west plus $5 million and other benefits. Elias Boudinot wrote, "we can see strong reasons to justify the actions of a minority . . . to do what the majority *would* do if they understood their condition."[26] Although the signers thought they were doing the best thing for their country, they were well aware of being just seventy-five out of fifteen thousand. They expected an angry response from fellow Cherokees. As old Major Ridge signed, he is reported to have said, "I have signed my death warrant."[27]

Andrew Jackson was delighted with the treaty. He knew it would convince some people, including powerful senators, that the Cherokee really did want to move west. It would allow him to get them out of their valuable homeland at last.

Chapter 4

The Trail of Tears

A hundred and fifty years after the Cherokee were forced from the southern Appalachians to Oklahoma, one man of Cherokee descent revisited the old captial of New Echota. "My whole body chills," he wrote in his journal, "as I face once again the fact that an entire nation—or those who survived—was moved to another part of the country like wild horses to the dog food company."[28] The Cherokee were not the only Native Americans to be forced west of the Mississippi by the Indian Removal Act of 1830. Tribes from Florida to the Great Lakes were also made to move. But the Cherokee's experience was so terrible and so unjust that their term for the journey, literally "the path where they cried," became the name given to the whole removal process: The Trail of Tears. The Trail was a horrible and unforgettable turning point in Cherokee history.

"The Name of This Nation Will Stink to the World"

From the moment they learned about the Treaty of New Echota, John Ross and most other Cherokee leaders fought it, with the hope that it would not be approved by the Senate. They rushed petitions to Washington proving that over fifteen thousand out of eighteen thousand Cherokee did not want the treaty. Some powerful members of the Senate, including Henry Clay, Daniel Webster, and John C. Calhoun, fought to turn the treaty down. When their effort failed by one vote, outrage boiled over in the press. Ralph Waldo Emerson, the greatest American literary voice of his day, wrote to President Martin Van Buren that most Americans were horrified at the government's action: "Sir, does the government think the people of the United States are become savage and mad? . . . You, sir, will bring down that chair on which you sit; and the name of this nation . . . will stink to the world."[29]

To President Van Buren, who had followed after Jackson, the Treaty of New Echota was a convenient excuse to get rid of the Cherokee. General James E. Wool was put in charge of enrolling and moving the tribe by the 1838 deadline.

In 1838, the U.S. government began to forcibly send the Cherokee on the long trek from Georgia to Oklahoma, called the Trail of Tears.

Wool, however, found that the job left a bitter taste in his mouth. He was surprised at first to discover that the Cherokee did not want to leave, and would not leave voluntarily. At the same time, it was clear that the people were fighting a losing battle against the whites who wanted their land. "If I could," Wool wrote, "I would remove every Indian tomorrow beyond the reach of the white men, who like vultures, are watching, ready to pounce upon their prey and strip them of everything they have."[30]

In spite of the army's efforts, only about two thousand Cherokee signed up to move before 1838. Most of these were supporters of removal and included many wealthy and mixed-blood families. They traveled in groups of several hundred, with their possessions, animal herds, and slaves. Some traveled over land and others moved by boat via the Tennessee, Ohio, Mississippi, and Arkansas Rivers. Just across the Arkansas border, in Indian Territory, they joined the Cherokee who had moved westward earlier in the century. The newcomers found land to farm and built houses among these "Old Settlers." The journey westward was not comfortable, even for these pro-removal families. A few died along the way from sickness and accidents. However, the combination of personal wealth and government aid meant most people were well fed and safely sheltered. Army officers led and supervised the large groups.

As the deadline of May 1838 approached, it became clear that the vast majority of Cherokee would not move unless forced. Sick at the prospect, General Wool resigned his post. Winfield Scott was named to supervise the ousting of the people. On May 10, he spoke to a large gathering of Cherokee, and had his words reprinted and spread throughout the territory: "Chiefs, head-men, warriors! Will you then, by resistance, compel us to resort to arms? . . . I am an old warrior, and I have been present at many a scene of slaughter; but spare me, I beseech you, the horror of witnessing the destruction of the Cherokees."[31]

Imprisonment in the Stockades

General Scott's plan was to sweep the Cherokee into stockades, and from there to three large camps near the Tennessee River, the departure point for the West. Soldiers were put to work building the needed stockades—large,

The Story of Tsali

Among the fugitives trying to evade removal from North Carolina were family groups headed by Cherokee named Euchella and Tsali. The story of Tsali has survived among the eastern Cherokee, changing in the retelling like other folk stories. One version of the story of Tsali was incorporated into a play presented by the eastern Cherokee beginning in the 1950s, called *Unto These Hills*. In the play, Tsali is presented as a hero. His family kills a few soldiers in an escape attempt. Then the weary army offers to let other fugitive Cherokee stay in the mountains if the guilty men will surrender. Tsali gives himself up. As a final blow, the army forces other Cherokee to execute him. From this tragedy the Eastern Band, still in existence today, is born.

The real story of Tsali is more complicated. Soldiers did capture Tsali and his family in the mountains and began to march them out. Tsali's teenaged son, Wa-

sitani, said later that Tsali's wife fell from an army horse when it started and she dropped her baby, who died when it struck the ground. Soon after, one of the family men pulled a hidden hatchet from his clothing and planted it in one soldier's head. A second soldier was killed by another blow as the Cherokee escaped. An angry General Scott ordered that Tsali's band be caught and killed.

Euchella was afraid that Tsali's actions had made all Cherokee look treacherous and that the army would take his family away. So, when army officers asked him for help, he felt he had to cooperate. In short order, Euchella's warriors and some allies captured and shot Tsali and several of his sons. Wasitani was spared only because of his youth. Then, since the Indians themselves had pursued, captured, and punished Tsali's band, the colonel in charge permitted them to stay in the mountains.

unroofed enclosures surrounded by pointed, upright log walls. Meanwhile, Scott stationed soldiers throughout Cherokee lands, and they began to round people up. The resistance he feared never occurred. Instead, most Cherokee kept on with their daily lives, unable to believe their leaders would fail and they would actually be forced to move. John G. Burnett, a soldier who took part in the removal, described what happened in his memoirs:

Men working in the fields were arrested and driven to the stockades. Women were dragged from their homes by soldiers whose language they could not understand. Children were often separated from their parents and driven into the stockades with the sky for a blanket and the earth for a pillow. And often the old and infirm were prodded with bayonets to hasten them to the stockades.[32]

A newspaper reporter wrote: "The captors sometimes drove the people with whooping and bellowing, like cattle through rivers, allowing them no time even to take off their shoes and stockings. Many, when arrested, were not so much as permitted to gather up their clothes."[33]

According to the Treaty of New Echota, the Cherokee were to be paid for their improvements on the land: houses, barns, mills, orchards, and animals. In some cases, these were properly valued and paid for. Most often, however, they were sold for almost nothing or simply taken. A rabble of whites followed the army to snatch up Indian posessions, set fire to cabins, and even rob Cherokee family graves of silver and other valuable ornaments.

Inside the stockades, as one Cherokee family story says, "the mud was deep, there wasn't much food, no one had anything to cover themselves with."[34] People were forced to stay at the stockades for weeks as they grew more and more crowded. Diseases spread easily, including measles, whooping cough, pleurisy, and fevers. By June, General Scott announced he had nearly all the Cherokee in thirteen stockades and three large riverside camps. However, even as Scott began to start groups on the westward journey, some Cherokee remained at large.

The People Who Stayed

Deep in ancient Cherokee country, in the high Smoky Mountains of North Carolina, about eleven hundred Cherokee people managed to evade the removal. About eight hundred of these were known as the Oconaluftee Cherokee because they had settlements along the Oconaluftee River, a tributary of the Tennessee. In that location years before, Chief Yonaguska (Drowning Bear) led his people to turn away from alcohol. His band decided in 1819 to become citizens of North Carolina, accept money from the government for their former Cherokee land, and leave the Cherokee government. Before 1836, the Oconaluftee got permission to stay where they were as state citizens.

One reason why the Oconaluftee Cherokee were able to keep their homes was that the area was not very valuable to whites: There was no gold, and the farms were steep, rough, and hard to reach through the forest. Because the region was so remote, it attracted refugees when the roundup of Cherokee began in 1838. Several hundred fugitives survived there. A white trader and friend named Will Thomas used Cherokee money to buy land for the Cherokee in his name. Land could still not be purchased and held in the names of Indians.

As the army departed from the area, the Oconaluftee and the fugitives settled into a quiet life based largely on ancient Cherokee ways: subsistence farming, hunting, and gathering. The group of about seventy families intermarried and spoke the Cherokee language. Isolated in the mountains, this group kept many aspects of Cherokee culture alive until after the Civil War.

The Trail of Tears Begins

Back at the stockades and camps along the Tennessee, the army spent the summer of 1838 getting groups started on their way west. Most were taken by steamer down the Tennessee and Ohio Rivers to the far side of the Mississippi, where Cape Girardeau is now located; then they continued overland through Missouri to the Indian Territory. Scenes of departure were often chaotic. As one newspaper reported,

> then came the shipping off to the west. The agent endeavored to induce the people to go into the boats voluntarily; but none would agree to go. The agent then struck a line through

Will Thomas

In *The Cherokee Indian Nation,* edited by Duane H. King, author Richard W. Iobst tells of a white North Carolinian who became a good friend to the Cherokee.

As a young man in the 1820s, Will Thomas got a job as clerk in the trading post at Qualla, one of the towns on the Oconaluftee. Fatherless, he was befriended by Chief Yonaguska, and eventually adopted by him, under the name of 'Will-Usdi': Little Will. Will learned to speak fluent Cherokee and soon became a trader in his own right for the band. The Oconaluftee people, unable to hold title to land as Indians, had their land put in Will's name, and he continued to buy parcels of land for Cherokees for years. By 1835, Will Thomas was acting as their spokesperson, attorney, and trade representative. Thomas shuttled many times to Washington and to the North Carolina capital at Raleigh to make sure his friends were not forced west. Then he worked tirelessly to get them the money they were owed under treaty provisions. Although he made a living as a trader to the Cherokee, it seems clear that Thomas worked so hard for them because he thought it was right: "The Indians are as much entitled to their rights as I am to mine," he wrote to a friend.

☀ A Child's Memory of Removal

Rebecca Neugin was a very young child when she and her family joined the Trail of Tears. The following is part of her memory of it, retold years later to historian Grant Foreman and reprinted in Theda Perdue and Michael D. Green's *The Cherokee Removal: A Brief History With Documents.*

"When the soldiers came to our house my father wanted to fight, but my mother told him that the soldiers would kill him if he did and we surrendered without a fight. They drove us out of our house to join other prisoners in a stockade. After they took us away my mother begged them to let her go back and get some bedding. So they let her go back and she brought what bedding and a few cooking utensils she could carry and had to leave behind all our other household possessions. My father had a wagon pulled by two spans of oxen to haul us in. Eight of my brothers and sisters and two or three widow women and children rode with us. . . . My mother and father walked all the way. . . . There was much sickness among the emigrants and a great many little children died of whooping cough."

the camp;—the soldiers rushed in and drove the devoted victims [those on one side of the line] into the boats, regardless of the cries and agonies of the poor helpless sufferers. In this cruel work, the most painful separations of families occurred.— Children were sent off and parents left, and so of other relations.[35]

In the heat of the summer, and weakened already by their confinement in the stockades, many Cherokee fell ill and died—especially of "flux," a term for severe diarrhea with blood and mucus. Horrified, the Cherokee National Council appealed to the government to allow the Cherokee to remove themselves to the West in the fall, after the season of humid heat had passed. One group appealed personally to General Scott: "We do not want to see our wives and children die. We do not want to die ourselves and leave them widows and orphans. We are in trouble sir our hearts are very heavy. The darkness of night is before us."[36]

The "darkness of night" certainly meant the threat of death. But to any Cherokee, the phrase would also have called up a complex of ideas centered around the ancient belief that west is the direction of blackness and of death, the location of the portal to the "darkening land" or "nightland" where spirits go after people die.

General Scott finally agreed to the Cherokee request, although he managed to send about three thousand west that summer. Far fewer than that actually arrived, due partly to deaths and partly to some large-scale escapes. One estimate was that no more than two thousand arrived in Indian Territory.

"We Are About to Take Our Final Leave"

The remaining thirteen thousand Cherokee were to move out in the fall of 1838 under the supervision of members of their own tribe. The Cherokee National Council met at Rattlesnake Springs, on the Tennessee River, to arrange for the trip. They resolved to keep the same constitution and laws in their new home, a matter of some importance when they arrived.

The population was divided into thirteen groups of roughly a thousand each. Each group was under the direction of a leader, with guides, wagon masters, blacksmiths, farriers to shoe horses, men to distribute food, two doctors, and members of the Cherokee Light Horse to help police the lines. The government provided one wagon per twenty people, one horse per four, and money with which to buy food for the road for eighty days—more than enough, it was estimated, for the trip. The plan for nearly all these people was to go overland, through Tennessee, Kentucky, Illinois, and Missouri to Indian Territory.

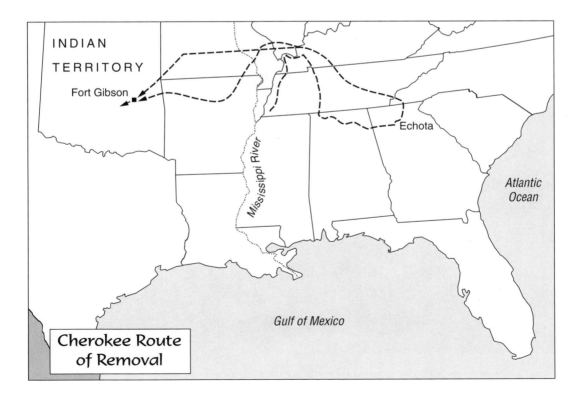

Cherokee Route of Removal

From the very beginning, though, things went wrong. Departure, scheduled to begin September 1, had to be postponed a month due to drought in the late summer. The groups traveled on roads, but with the first rains and the first dozen wagons rutting them, the roads became treacherous and deep in mud. Suppliers of food sold bad goods to the Cherokee, thinking no one would be able to do anything about it: moldy hay for the horses, wormy cornmeal, rotten meat. In some cases, leaders were forced to burn the meat before their people caught sight of it, they were hungry enough to eat even food so spoiled it was sure to make them sick. Illnesses compounded by camp life and bad food meant that space was taken in wagons by the sick. Old people often had to walk, and provisions and posessions were left behind. White traders exchanged whiskey for the Indians' valued belongings; toll collecters and ferrymen overcharged.

The worst part of the journey for many Cherokee, though, was undoubtedly the wrench of leaving home. George Hicks wrote back to John Ross as his group was about to leave Cherokee territory,

We are now about to take our final leave and kind farewell to our native land, the country that the great spirit

The Cherokee National Council meets to arrange for the trip west.

gave our Fathers; we are on the eve of leaving that country that gave us birth . . . it is with sorrow that we are forced by the authority of the white man to quit the scenes of our childhood. . . . [W]e bid a final farewell to it and all we hold dear.[37]

Elijah Hicks, conducting another group, wrote of their depression, "the people are very loth [reluctant] to go on, and unusually slow in preparing for starting each morning. I am not surprised at this because they are moving not from choice to an unknown region not desired by them. I am disposed to make full allowance for their unhappy movement."[38]

Hicks's group had to pause at Hopkinsville, Kentucky, to bury the old and respected Chief White Path. The flag they raised over his grave served as a symbol of the broken connection with Cherokee lands and ancestors to each group that followed on the trail.

The Trail in Winter

Winter came on quickly in 1838. Many Cherokee were lightly dressed and had only canvas tents to keep out the weather. Private John Burnett, who accompanied one group, remembered,

On the morning of November 17th we encountered a terrific sleet and snow storm with freezing temperatures and that day . . . the sufferings of the Cherokees were awful. The trail of the exiles was a trail of death. . . . They had to sleep in the wagons and on the ground without fire. And I have known as many as twenty-two . . . to die in one night of pneumonia.[39]

Principal Chief John Ross, last to depart with a small contingent in November, had to leave his group because his wife Quatie grew seriously ill. He took her by boat, but she died of pneumonia before reaching Indian Territory.

Perhaps the harshest experience along the Trail of Tears was the crossing of the Mississippi River. Before most Cherokee could get across, "a blast of frigid air from the north swept the river area and overnight froze the surface of the river. . . . The horses walked round and round a turntable, winding the ropes that pulled the boat across and back. The ice prevented them from getting a footing and floating ice jammed the boat."[40]

There was no choice but to camp and wait for the freeze to thaw. Other groups of Cherokee, who had been several days behind, bumped up against those already stranded at the river, and huge camps of thousands spread across the frozen ground. "I am afraid," wrote Evan Jones, leader of one of the groups, "that with all the care that can be exercised . . . there will be an immense amount of suffering, and loss of life."[41] In fact, pneumonia and exposure took many there, especially the very young and the old, as time stretched on. Rev. Jesse Bushyhead reported that his group had to wait a month to cross the Mississippi.

As winter went on, the Cherokee limped across Missouri. A memory repeated in Oklahoma today says that barefoot Cherokee left tracks of blood in the snow. Their

The Trail of Tears was especially difficult in the winter, where many died from the cold and illness.

starving dogs fought one another to lick at the tracks.

The last of the Cherokee forced west straggled into their new territory between January and March of 1839. Some had taken as long as six months to make a trip that some pro-removal Cherokee had made in good weather within one month. The Old Settlers and the Removal Party Cherokee were there to greet the last of their tribe to arrive. But the newcomers had to begin their lives anew, in poor health and spirits and in a strange place with few resources. Many more died in the first hard months after arriving in Indian Territory. Today, no one knows exactly how many Cherokee died on the Trail of Tears. Most historians estimate the toll at four thousand. A recent statistical estimate, based on the natural increase of the population before removal, places the death count at more than twice that many.

Chapter 5

In the New Lands

Dawn, June 22, 1839: A group of twenty-five Cherokee men ride up to the house of John Ridge, leader of the pro-removal group. They pull the sleeping Ridge from his bed to the yard, where they stab him twenty-five times, then ritually walk over his body one by one. A short time later, another band of thirty Cherokee catches Elias Boudinot outside the mission where he is assisting and tomahawk him in the head many times. At ten o'clock that morning, yet another group waylays Major Ridge, the third important pro-removal leader. They shoot him from his horse.

These three murders expressed the bitterness of people torn from their homeland, impoverished, mourning their many dead. Someone, they felt, had to take the blame and be punished. The enmity driven home on that day, which was to haunt the Cherokee Nation for decades to come, had its roots in the Treaty of New Echota and fed on the resentments created when survivors of the Trail of Tears reached their destination.

The Cherokee Divided

The Trail of Tears ended at more than eight thousand square miles of new Cherokee land located just west of the Arkansas and Missouri borders in what is now northwestern Oklahoma. As in the East, Cherokee owned the land in common, but individuals claimed parts of it for their farms, homes, and businesses. In the new lands, the rule was "first come, first served": Whoever got to a choice location first could claim it.

The first choice of land had gone to the group called the Old Settlers, Cherokees who had left the Appalachians at various times between the 1790s and 1830s to make a new life in the West. The second group to arrive were members of the relatively wealthy Removal Party. These people, including the chief signers of the Treaty of New Echota, arrived in 1837 and found there were still good farmlands to be had. "In a few years," John Ridge wrote, "it will be the garden spot of the United States."[42] He and his father, Major

Tahlequah in 1841

Following the Trail of Tears, Cherokee did their best to rebuild. In 1841, a visitor named Ethan Hitchcock saw the Nation's effort and wrote in his journal about the Cherokee tradition of providing food for the hungry. Here he is quoted in *The Cherokee Removal: A Brief History with Documents*, edited by Theda Perdue and Michael D. Green.

"As we approached Tahlequah we met several persons riding out, two women among them, well dressed and covered with shawls, the men well dressed with hats and all were riding good horses. These people, said I, don't look very wild. . . . As we came in sight of the capital, I saw a number of log houses arranged in order with streets; or one street at all events, was clearly visible but the houses were very small . . . —we saw a number of people. 'There are cooks, public cooks we call them,' said [Hitchcock's escort, Cherokee officer John] Drew, 'along those houses, meat, etc., is furnished to them and they cook for the public. Everybody can go to the picnic tables. See there,' said he, 'you can see some eating dinner,' I saw some 20 at one table. 'The nation pays the expense.'"

Ridge, both farmed and set up a store where other Cherokee could buy what they needed to begin afresh. The Ridge store offered credit to people without money, and soon many families were in debt to them.

When the majority of the tribe arrived from the Trail of Tears, the newcomers were officially welcomed, but they noticed that the best land had already been claimed. To buy goods, they had to go into debt to white traders or to the Ridges, men who had "betrayed" the nation with the Treaty of New Echota. Worst of all, they felt that the government they had brought with them, the government of the majority, was not recognized by the other groups. And many suspected that leaders of the Removal Party were working with the Old Settlers to deny rights to the newcomer majority.

A Violent Time

The murders of the Ridges and Boudinot had been planned and carried out within days of the first council meeting between Old Settlers and new arrivals. The killers claimed they had acted lawfully under an 1829 Cherokee law which ordered death to anyone who sold or traded away tribal land without the permission of the National Council. Even though Principal Chief John Ross had known nothing about the plans for the murders, he and his council did not prosecute the killers. This inaction led to bitterness, which eventually was expressed in a new wave of violence. The outbursts peaked in 1845 with a series of revenge killings, robberies, and vandalism. Probably a major reason for the social chaos was the Cherokee's feeling of homelessness, rootlessness, and lack of meaning in life. "I am so tired of living this way," wrote one Cherokee woman. "It has wore my spirits out just the thought of not having a good home. I am so perfectly sick of the world."[43] Some drank whiskey to forget, and some fell into despair. But some lashed out at real and imagined enemies.

The downward spiral of 1845 reached a low point when Stand Watie, brother of the murdered Elias Boudinot, took over an old fort; war seemed possible. Representatives of the Removal Party, Old Settlers, and the Ross party rushed to Washington, D.C., to try to get support. President James Polk announced he was ready to divide up the Cherokee land among the three groups in order to stop the violence. This proposal brought everyone to their senses. The Cherokee began to talk to each other in Washington and finally reached agreement. They offered President Polk a new treaty in which money due to the Cherokee from the United States under the removal treaty would be distributed to all; claims among the groups were settled. The

Stand Watie, who took over a fort and threatened war on the Cherokee for the murder of his brother.

president signed gladly. Even Stand Watie told reporters, "I intend to be peaceable."[44]

Making a New Living

The new land was very different from the land the Cherokee had left behind. A federal agent said of the new Cherokee acres, "at least two-thirds are entirely unfit for cultivation. A large share of the tillable land is of an inferior quality. Most of the untillable land is entirely worthless, even for timber, as it consists of stony ridges and valleys covered with a scrubby growth."[45]

Cherokee land in the East had been very fertile in the river valleys, and well watered. Here, the tough grass fought the plow and droughts ruined harvests. Difficult as it was, poor families planted crops and built cabins. The ethic of clan support and community sharing, long a part of Cherokee life, helped sustain many newcomers. Cherokee traditions of ceremony and healing were continued, although with difficulty. The awe-inspiring mountain peaks had been replaced by low hills. The sacred locations of ancient myths were far away. Even many plants traditionally used by the priests to heal and bring forces into balance could not be found in the new land.

For a few hundred Cherokee families, adjusting was easier. These were the wealthiest people. They could afford work animals and field hands. As they had in their homeland, the wealthy Cherokee farmers used slave labor, and more slaves generally meant better harvests.

By 1850, prosperity was definitely increasing for most Cherokee. The capital city, Tahlequah, attracted trade and the business generated by the tribal government. Park Hill, a town to the south of Tahlequah, became a social and cultural center. A new national newspaper, the *Cherokee Advocate,* had begun publication in Cherokee and English in 1844. Thirty-eight Protestant churches or mission stations dotted the land. A tribally sponsored public school system was also started in

the 1840s. Chief Ross and the Council hoped it would bring economic well-being to all Cherokee, to the relatively impoverished traditional Cherokee as well as those already thriving.

The "Full-Bloods" and the "Mixed-Bloods"

"Those who have little Cherokee blood, in comparing themselves with white men, glory in being 'Cherokee,' " wrote a missionary, "yet [they] look with contempt upon those who speak Cherokee only or chiefly as 'Indians.' "[46] This odd state of affairs was due to the fact that the people found themselves in two social classes with different ideas of what it ought to mean to be Cherokee. Nearly all the wealthiest people of the tribe had some European ancestry. They were fiercely proud of being Cherokee, but they were eager to prove that the Cherokee could do everything other people could do. They wanted the tribe to "advance," and to them, this meant imitating other Americans in wealth, knowledge, and institutions. They themselves lived like members of the American planter class, and they set the Cherokee public school system to mirror their ideals. The schools were to educate in English only and to prepare students for a life as prosperous as any of their non-Indian neighbors.

Even though this elite ruled through the 1850s, it was always a minority. Most Cherokee were "full-bloods," who spoke and wrote only Cherokee. Only a handful were illiterate. Most full Cherokee were subsistence farmers who followed many old traditions of the tribe, including hunting, ball play, ceremonies, and all-night dances. They still depended on the *adonisgi* (priests) for healing, relief from drought, and help with personal problems and foretelling the future. By the 1850s, most full Cherokee also considered themselves Christian. They attended churches and mission stations, and were especially fond of religious camp meetings. These open-air meetings, which lasted for days, fit in with the Cherokee love of social occasions in which the whole community could assemble over a long period of time.

Full-Cherokee children were often kept away from the public schools, where the English language made learning difficult and teachers often did not approve of their way of life. Many families chose to teach their children traditional skills such as hunting and use of wild plants at home. Once children learned the syllabary, they could read the Bible (translated by missionaries) and the *Cherokee Advocate*. They could keep up with the business of their nation, since all speeches were translated into both English and Cherokee.

The Keetoowah Society

In the 1850s, many full Cherokee joined a secret society called Keetoowah (also spelled Kituwah), named after the Cherokee's most ancient town in the Appalachians, a sacred place of tribal origin. The name "Keetoowah" was also used for an old society, perhaps of priests, dedicated to preserving the beliefs and rituals of the

A Petition from a Black Cherokee

Freedmen in Cherokee territory fought for their civil rights through petitions like this one (spelling regularized) sent by Louis Rough to President Ulysses Grant and reprinted in William G. McLoughlin's *After the Trail of Tears: The Struggle for Cherokee Sovereignty, 1839–1880*.

"Mr. Grant . . . The Cherokees says they ain't in favor of the black man having any claim, that they had rather any body else have a right than us poor blacks. . . . Downing [Principal Chief] is for us, Ochalata, and Mr. Sixkiller, them three is in our favor, but what can they do with so many [on the other side]? . . . We all don't think it right too, after we have made them rich and built their land, do you? . . . Now Mister Grant, I want a message from [you] right away. . . . Please give me a little information what the dark population is to do about these school funds to have our Children educated [?] Are we to raise them up like heathens [?]"

tribe. The full-bloods chose the name for their society deliberately to suggest that they too wanted to preserve the knowledge and life ways of the Cherokee, which were under threat. The society's most important purpose, however, was to challenge the Cherokee slaveholding planters who were in charge of the tribal government.

Part of the political aim of the Keetoowahs had to do with their religious opposition to slavery. The society's leaders were northern Baptists. Missionaries from their church encouraged them to fight the institution of slavery and the system that supported it. According to Keetoowah leader Budd Gritts, "It was plain to be seen [in 1858] that the Cherokee people,

The First Cherokee Battle of the Civil War

The Cherokee fought in the Civil War for the first time when a Creek leader, Opothleyholo, called on Creek and other Indians to join him in fighting slaveholders. Confederate officers were afraid he would spark a slave revolt all over the region, and they asked Cherokee troops to help fight him. Warriors under Col. John Drew arrived at the scene, but once they saw what was going on, some 420 out of 480 deserted and went to fight on Opothleyholo's side. A disgusted Stand Watie then arrived with his company of Confederate Cherokee to carry on the fight. Already, to the horror of many in the Nation, Cherokee were fighting Cherokee.

without a full understanding, were taking sides with the South. . . . I was then and there appointed to devise some plan that would be best for the Cherokee people and should place us [the nonslaveholding majority] in control of the Cherokee government."[47] The political organizing of the Keetoowahs worked. By 1861, traditional Cherokee were in control of the National Council at Tahlequah.

The Cherokee Choose Sides

The Civil War loomed like a storm cloud over the western Cherokee in 1861. The Council and Chief Ross had resisted siding with the Confederacy of the southern states or with the Union. Yet in that year, all the other Indian tribes in the Territory had declared loyalty to the Confederacy. So had Arkansas, the Cherokee's nearest state neighbor. The Union had withdrawn all its troops from Indian Territory and was withholding the yearly payment to the Cherokee. To top it all off, Confederate general Ben McCulloch made Stand Watie, Ross's old enemy, a colonel in the Confederate army. Three hundred Cherokee men were armed to serve under Watie.

In alarm, Chief Ross called a Council meeting in August. He had decided that the best path for the nation was to join the Confederates. He presented the idea as the only way to keep the Cherokee together. "As Brothers live; as Brothers die!"[48] he urged. Slavery and other matters were not as important as unity. The best chance for unity and the safety of their homes seemed to lie in taking sides with their nearest neighbors and fellow tribes. Though many at the meeting were confused about the meaning of the vote, Ross convinced the Council to approve his proposal. He immediately made an agreement with the Confederates.

The Horror of War

The Cherokee remained officially pro-Confederate through the great Battle of Pea Ridge, Arkansas, in 1862. At Pea Ridge, Cherokee soldiers were mowed down in a decisive Union victory. A few months later, a Union regiment entered Cherokee land. Chief Ross was taken east to Washington, and Stand Watie named himself Principal Chief at Tahlequah. The period that followed was chaotic. As Watie's troops struggled with pro-Union Cherokee, factions raided one another, burned homes, and destroyed crops.

When the war ended in 1865, officials in Washington were not inclined to be merciful to tribes that had fought against them. The United States declared that all former treaties with the Cherokee were at an end. A new treaty signed in 1866 gave to Kansas a large section of northeastern Cherokee-owned territory called the Neutral Lands. The treaty forced a thousand Delaware and seven hundred Shawnee onto Cherokee lands and made them

Chief John Ross convinced the Cherokee tribal government to side with the Confederacy during the Civil War.

Cherokee citizens. Railroad companies, which had long had an eye on Cherokee country, were granted rights of way to cross the land.

Chief John Ross died at age seventy-five just before the treaty was signed. Stand Watie, who had achieved the rank of general in the Confederate army, died a few years later. The Cherokee population was reduced by about a quarter from all the effects of the Civil War: deaths in battle as well as deaths from exposure and disease. The remaining fifteen thousand people, including twelve hundred war orphans, faced what one observer called a "blackened and desolate waste"[49] where their settlements had been.

Beginning Again— Once Again

Just as they did after the American Revolution, and as they did after the Trail of Tears, the Cherokee started over in spite of the tremendous shock they had endured. Under the treaty signed at the end of the war, people the Cherokee had held as slaves were accepted as citizens of the tribe. They were able to farm and vote, though they were denied some rights, such as the right to send their children to any public school. Separate schools for black children were established in some places.

The lack of slaves on Cherokee plantations meant the owners had to find other ways to make their land pay. Some of the planters attracted white farmers to work their land by selling them permits. The permits had been intended as a means of securing skilled non-Cherokee to work on Cherokee land when there was a need. But now these documents were used to allow whites to gain a foothold on Cherokee farmland. Many of these "guest workers" had hopes of claiming the land for themselves in the future.

Most Cherokee families rebuilt their small farms and raised animals. John B. Jones, one of the missionaries who had encouraged the Keetoowah Society, became a U. S. agent sympathetic to the tribe. He described ordinary Cherokee houses in 1871 as "equal to the best hewn-log houses in the Southwestern states. . . . Many families have large double-houses, a storey and a half high, with hall between, and all necessary outbuildings."[50]

Businesses and White Intruders

Many Cherokee felt that future prosperity lay in manufacturing and business. The frontier was closing, and industry was growing rapidly in the last half of the nineteenth century. The problem for the tribe, however, was lack of money to get businesses started. Nearly everyone in the nation was in debt, and outside investors were unwilling to lend money to Indians. The federal government did not help, either. When the Cherokee and their Five Tribes neighbors suggested starting their own railroad through their territory, Congress refused even to consider a bill giving them permission.

Meanwhile, white businesses entered Cherokee territory and used its resources. Cattle drives from Texas passed through on their way to northern railheads. Just as the Cherokee started to tax the drives, railroads came through and promised to stop the drives. Railroad builders cut valuable trees and killed livestock, paying for only a small amount of the damage.

Perhaps the worst aspect of the coming of the railroads was the fact that Congress promised the companies a large amount of Indian land whenever Indian control might end. That promise caused railroad executives to work continually to get Congress to end the Cherokee Nation and its tribal neighbors. One congressman wrote, "And now these soulless corporations hover, like greedy cormorants over this Territory and incite Congress to remove all restraints and allow them to sweep down and swallow over 23 million acres of the land."[51]

The Drive Toward Allotment

The railroads wanted tribal rule in Indian Territory to end. They proposed that individual Indians be given a certain amount of land each, and that the rest of the land be handed to the railroads or made available for settlement. This process, called "allotment," was designed precisely to end tribal land ownership. Since tribal government without tribal land was considered pointless, allotment would have the effect of destroying the government of any tribe that participated.

Many well-meaning Americans thought allotment would benefit Indians. Senator Henry L. Dawes of Massachusetts spoke about common ownership of tribal land:

> They have got as far as they can go, because they own their land in common . . . and under that there is no enterprise to make your home any better than your neighbors. There is no selfishness, which is at the bottom of civilization. Till this people will consent to give up their lands, and divide them among their citizens so that each can own the land he cultivates, they will not make much more progress.[52]

A Business Effort Fails

One Cherokee who tried to get a manufacturing business started after the Civil War ended up showing others that they would not be allowed to succeed for long at the expense of non-Indian competitors. E. C. Boudinot, nephew of Stand Watie, borrowed money from his uncle to produce chewing tobacco plugs from Cherokee-grown tobacco. Under an old treaty, Cherokee were supposed to be able to sell their produce without paying U. S. tax, and Boudinot thought he could undersell his rivals in surrounding states. The Watie and Boudinot Tobacco Company built a factory and did well for a short time until rival companies brought them to federal court. The court decided the treaty provision was meaningless. Boudinot lost his business to taxes and was even charged criminally.

In 1887, a bill written by Dawes made allotment the law. The Cherokee and other Five Nations tribes argued strongly against the Dawes Act, and so at first they were granted an exception. However, pressures for allotment grew stronger daily in Indian Territory. Part of the pressure came from white people who wanted the land, but part of it came from people who were upset at the lawlessness that had grown since the Civil War. Indian Territory had become a refuge for criminals trying to avoid federal and state law enforcement. Besides, disputes over land use often went unsettled in a muddle of confusing laws and clogged tribal courts. Allotment promised to bring in the standardized laws and procedures being used in the rest of the country.

Allotment Becomes Inevitable

A minority of Cherokee favored allotment, both for reasons of safety and because they hoped to make more money by buy-ing or selling land. Most pro-allotment Cherokee were wealthy members of the old southern group.

By far the greatest number of Cherokee opposed allotment, but unlike some other tribes, they chose to work nonviolently. The Keetoowah Society reorganized in 1889 to work against allotment and the end of Cherokee self-rule.

Cherokee power began to wane when the U. S. government declared the western part of the old Indian Territory to be the

Many Natives fought against allotment, but some supported the idea in hopes of making a greater profit on land shares.

Vastly in debt, the Cherokee were forced to sell large tracts of land to the federal government for use by white settlers.

Oklahoma Territory. The Cherokee sold vast areas to the federal government for very little money. Soon a series of land "runs" began in which country formerly in Indian hands was opened to white settlement. The Cherokee, still heavily in debt, sold two large tracts called the Cherokee Outlet and the Cherokee Strip, partly to gain money and partly because they thought that if they did not, the land would soon be taken anyway.

The great blow to the Cherokee Nation came in 1898, when Congress passed the Curtis Act. It ended Cherokee government, abolished Cherokee laws and courts, and placed the people under U. S. law, which at the time denied Indians citizenship, including the right to vote.

Chapter 6

Twentieth-Century Cherokee

The phoenix is a mythical bird which burns to death periodically, yet rises from the ashes to live again. The story of the phoenix has reminded many Cherokee of the history of their own people, and for that reason the first tribal newspaper, launched in the 1820s, was called the *Phoenix*. In the last hundred years, the Cherokee have again seemed phoenix-like. The first decade of the twentieth century was perhaps the lowest point in their history. Yet by the final decade of the century, the Cherokee had adapted, re-grouped, and come to life once again from ashes—if in a somewhat different form.

The Dawes Commission Descends

From Washington, D.C., in 1895, a Cherokee delegation wrote home about the allotment law: "It did seem as if the world was about to rise in arms against us. . . . [M]any of the great dailies [newspapers] that a few years ago pleaded so persistently for the liberation of the slaves, are now insisting upon 'opening' our country for the settlement and occupancy of the whites."[53]

With the new law behind them, a group of officials called the Dawes Commission descended on Cherokee land to enroll tribe members and assign land to them. In Cherokee country, each head of household was to receive the equivalent of forty acres of average land as a homestead allotment, plus a varied amount of land as a "supplement." The process of dividing up the land caused havoc. New, straight property lines did not reflect long-established borders of farms and left no room for hunting grounds. Some Cherokee were given land far distant from their homes, while others saw their old lands taken away. None of these problems were nearly as great, however, as the constant, overwhelming activity of land-grabbers eager to make money by honest or dishonest means.

The wealthier Cherokee came out of the process with the least loss. Robert Owen, for example, foresaw that his ten-thousand-acre estate would be divided for allotment. He arranged to have sections of it allotted to Cherokee people who lived at least one hundred miles away and did not want the property. Then he rented it back from them with contracts which forced them to sell him their allotments as soon as they legally could.

Cherokee people with less influence and less available cash could not make such arrangements. Many of the least-informed country people were actually rounded up by land agents and brought in by train to the enrollment office. There, for a small reward, they claimed and then immediately lost the land that was their due. Congress tried to protect full-blooded Cherokee by prohibiting sale of their land for some years after allotment. But land agents convinced some Cherokee to lease their land for pennies, with its sale to come later. Throughout Indian Territory, the agents who handled Indian land were called "grafters," which means people who use their position illegally and immorally to gain money or advantages. In the frenzy

The phoenix, a bird that periodically burns then rises from its own ashes, is the official symbol of the Cherokee Nation.

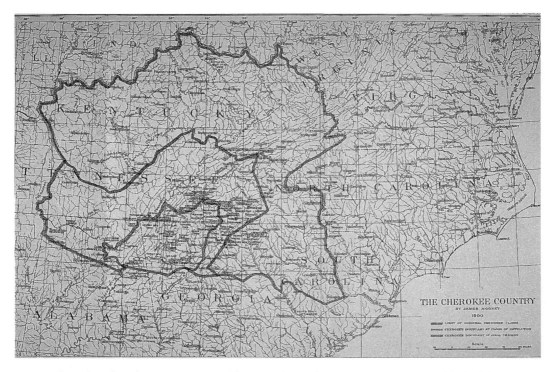

When the Cherokee were assigned land, property lines did not reflect established farm borders and there was no room left for hunting grounds.

of land deals, the word actually lost its negative quality; grafting and land dealing were the same thing.

In many places, no grafters were needed. White settlers simply took land with forged or false documents. Professional "guardians" also appeared to take legal charge of the property of orphans. They regularly kept for themselves most profits from timber sales and rental of the land. "The general effect of allotment," wrote historian Angie Debo, "was an orgy of plunder and exploitation probably unparalleled in American history."[54]

Some Cherokee Withdraw

Some traditional Cherokee refused to go along with allotment at all. In 1905, Redbird Smith led a group of Keetowahs to form a new society called the Nighthawk Keetoowahs. They refused to acknowledge allotment, refused titles to land, and retreated to their own settlements in the hills. What they were doing was part of the ancient Cherokee tradition of "withdrawl." If a minority could not agree with the majority's consensus, that minority had the right to withdraw from the council fire and not act in accord with the majority.

Other Indians in the Five Tribes also withdrew. Smith's group joined others in the "Four Mothers Society" to work toward returning to the old treaties and communal ownership of the land. Members of the Society appeared before a Senate committee to explain their point of view. Smith said,

> I can't stand and live and breathe if I take this allotment. Under the allotment rules I would see all around me . . . people who are ready to grab from under us my living and my home. If I would accept such a plan I would be going in starvation. To take and put the Indians on the land in severalty would be just the same as burying them, for they could not live.[55]

Invisible Cherokee

Oklahoma statehood in 1907 brought an official end to the government of the Cherokee Nation. The last Principal Chief, William Rogers, was allowed to remain in office until 1917, but his only power was that of signing land deeds on behalf of his people. After Rogers's death, the U. S. president appointed "chiefs" for the Cherokee, but these men had little power. Even though the new state had once been the refuge of Indians, so many whites had moved in that the population was only 5.3 percent Indian. The 31,400 Cherokee made up only a part of that percentage.

When allotment occurred, Redbird Smith attempted to fight it by starting his own society.

A few prominent Cherokee publicly identified themselves as Cherokee. Among tthem were Robert Owens, one of the first two senators from Oklahoma, and Will Rogers, who became famous as a comedian and actor in the 1920s. Wealthier and mixed-blood Cherokee tended to mix in with the general state population, however. Most of these people became "invisible" as Cherokee: No one could tell from their words or actions that they were of Cherokee heritage.

Other Cherokee seemed invisible because they lived far from cities; they were never in the news. They tried to live as they had before, though most were poorer than ever. Still, with support from family and clan, they managed to keep their language and traditions alive.

Land and Poverty for the Eastern Band.

Back in North Carolina, the Cherokee who had remained survived the Civil War, in which some of them fought on the Confederate side. After the war, their old friend and advocate Will Thomas lay gravely ill and in debt. What would happen to all the Cherokee land which was registered in his name? The land had been divided into districts or "towns" following the pattern of Cherokee settlement. But the towns had no official voice or government. In 1868, representatives from each of the towns met to form their own association with a constitution. The Eastern Band of Cherokee Indians officially came into being in 1870. Soon they faced their worst expectation: Thomas's creditors claimed his land in payment for debts due them.

The Cherokee Language

In *Living Stories of the Cherokee*, edited by Barbara R. Duncan, a contemporary speaker of Cherokee, Robert Bushyhead, talks about the sound of his language and why he values it.

"I have been commended in speaking the English language for the fact that I speak slowly and distinctly and clearly. And the Cherokee, when I speak that, that's the way Cherokee is set up—slow and distinct, and it has a flow. It has a rhythm that is beautiful. And once you lose that rhythm, then, of course, you're lost. For instance, if I say, 'Tomorrow, I'm going back to my home,' there's a rhythm to it. Someone has explained it in this way: It sounds like a waterfall—It's that melodious. One of the most important things is to hear sounds. And that's why the inflections are so important to me. . . . I believe for the Cherokee people, preserving our language is the most important. The language is a possession that was given us by the Great Spirit. Every effort should be made to retain the most important legacy we have, which was put in our trust."

Here, though, the federal government stepped in to help the Cherokee, suing for the land in court on behalf of the Eastern

had always really been Cherokee property—bought with Cherokee money, and occupied by them. The new tribal organization arranged to pay Thomas's creditors seven thousand dollars, and after that the land belonged to the Eastern Band. The government, however, decided to hold the land in trust for the Band, partly to protect the Indians and partly to control their activities. The same basic arrangement continues to this day, although Cherokee now have more self-governing powers on the fifty-two-thousand-acre reservation.

Though their land seemed safe at last, the eastern Cherokee fell on hard times after the Civil War. Increased settlement around them brought waves of European plant diseases, and insects caused serious crop destruction. Paying jobs became part of eastern Cherokee life for the first time around 1900 as some of the men were employed in cutting wood for pulp or working for the newly arrived railroad. However, these jobs were not enough to lift the community from poverty—especially in 1900, when a Cherokee earned thirty-five cents an hour on the same job that paid white workers one dollar an hour.

The problems of poverty were compounded by those of alcoholism. Alcohol used up family income and hampered a person's ability to work. Liquor was officially outlawed in the United States in the 1920s by the Eighteenth Amendment, and people found it increasingly difficult to buy alcohol from traders. But many Cherokee set up their own stills to make whiskey at home, and the problems continued. When the whole nation fell into economic depression in the 1930s, the Cherokee fell also—though they were already at the bottom of the heap.

The Family, the Gadugi, and the Great Smoky Mountains National Park

The eastern Cherokee were not completely overwhelmed by hard times, thanks to some institutions that had always served them well. First among these was the extended family. By the early twentieth century, many clan-related customs had faded, and some Cherokee did not even know which clan they were in. But close relations among extended family members remained. It was common through the 1940s for three generations to live in one house. Child care was shared, as were chores. People in distress felt comfortable calling on family members for help with money, illness, and other problems. Cherokee respect for elders ensured that the aged would be cared for, even if the young had to sacrifice for it. Cherokee women were generally the powerful heads of household, as they had been traditionally. Husbands, however, sometimes found it difficult to fit into the family pattern when they could not bring home a good income. Some left home for months or even years to work in distant states. Gambling and alcohol tempted others.

Just as family helped people get by, so did community. One formal way of sharing was the *gadugi,* a Cherokee word for a cooperative work association. Members met to labor on one another's farms in sequence. Like the Keetoowahs back in Oklahoma, they also took care of members who were ill, made loans to members, and helped with funerals. The *gadugi* is probably a remnant of the village organization which once gathered to plant and harvest for all the families of a chiefdom. Though formal *gadugis* did not exist after 1920, informal cooperative work groups continued at least through the 1960s, helping many Cherokee to get jobs done.

In 1934, when the Great Depression was at its height, the U.S. government created Great Smoky Mountains National Park. A road through the Eastern Band's reservation became a gateway to the park. Suddenly, a new economic mainstay came into being for the Cherokee: summer tourism. The town of Cherokee, North Carolina, mushroomed with tourist shops; the Eastern Band opened its own motel. Crafts cooperatives sprouted in which Cherokee wove baskets, made pottery, and created other items for the tourist trade. Older Cherokee

This Eastern Cherokee woman finger-weaves traditional cloth for sale.

At Tsa-La-Gi

Tsa-La-Gi (in Oklahoma) is a Cherokee heritage complex open to visitors interested in learning about the history of the tribe. It is owned and operated by the Cherokee Nation, as are a motel and gift shop a short distance away. The central attraction is a reconstructed village inside a timber palisade. There, Cherokee demonstrate crafts, including canoe building, basket making, and weaving. There is a blowgun demonstration and occasional ceremonial dance. In addition to the village, a national museum displays current Native American art. The Cherokee National Archives and Library are available to researchers. Also on the grounds is a theater in which the Trail of Tears outdoor drama is performed in summer.

Indians were especially affected by the tourist boom. Their skills and knowledge were in greater demand for craft making and storytelling. Income from these activities and from the newly established Social Security system helped the elders feel like less of a burden to their families.

Tourism also brought strains. Some shopkeepers had Cherokee ancestry, but some were "white Cherokees,"—outsiders or descendants of traders who had managed to get themselves officially counted as members of the tribe. These eager merchants had the cash to lease valuable shops, and they reaped the profit. A class division based on skin color continued to bedevil the Eastern Band for decades.

The Cherokee Nation, Reborn in the West

It was a strange twist of history that the Cherokee who stayed in the East without tribal land ended up with their own reservation, while the bulk of the tribe, which was forced west with a guarantee of land, ended up landless. In the 1920s and 1930s, American public opinion began to change about the way the Indians should be treated. The promise of the Dawes Act, that individual land ownership would lead Indians to prosperity, had not come true. A 1924 law giving Indians full citizenship did little to help, especially when many states ignored Indians' rights to serve on juries or even vote. In 1928, Congress received the Merriam Report, a survey of the conditions of life for Indians across the country. The report made it clear that allotment had resulted in poverty and unhappiness for most Indians.

The result, in time, was the Indian Reorganization Act of 1934. This law ended the allotment process, still dragging on in some places. It provided means for tribes to regain some land, money, and representation. Oklahoma managed to get itself exempted from the act, but passed its own weaker version. The Cherokee, divided and suspicious, were reluctant to form another tribal organization that might turn out to be only a tool of the federal government. At last, in 1948,

Chief Bartley Milam called a Cherokee convention. Government by an eleven-person council began. The new tribal organization was supposed to work for the social and economic well-being of the Cherokee. However, the Principal Chief was still presidentially appointed. In 1949, President Truman named a wealthy, mixed-blood oil executive, W.W. Keeler, to the post, and he held it for more than twenty years.

New Indian Pride

The 1960s and 1970s were years of social change in the United States—and among the Cherokee. In 1961, the courts ordered the government to pay the tribe $15 million for the Cherokee Outlet land, which had been taken long ago. The money helped promote tribal government projects, such as a national historical society with a model ancient village, museum, and Trail of Tears drama.

Beyond official events, the traditional Cherokee living in the Ozark hills gave birth to a new local organization. The "Five County Cherokees" were established in 1965 to defend hunting rights. In meeting together, this group found common cause in many fresh efforts. For instance, they built a new stomp dance ground, founded a Cherokee-language school, and criticized the model ancient village. An observer said, "The diversity of projects was incredible. The Cherokee country was in ferment."[56]

In 1971, the Cherokee finally gained the right to elect their own chief. A new

Wilma Mankiller, leader of the Cherokee Nation (left), and President Bill Clinton (right).

tribal constitution followed in 1976, and three years later the tribal offices moved into a sleek, modern complex south of Tahlequah, Oklahoma. The Cherokee Nation bought land, operated businesses, set up schools, and ran social aid programs. The new activism reached a peak in 1987 when the tribe elected its first female Principal Chief, Wilma Mankiller.

Improving Their Lives on Their Own

Members of the Cherokee Nation live in fourteen eastern Oklahoma counties, and vary from wealthy executives to backhills laborers. Most of them are not well off, however, and some remain extremely poor. The tribal government today serves as their complete self-help organization. The Nation has taken over the function of all federal programs affecting the Cherokee, including Head Start, public housing, Job Corps, courts, and drug and alcohol abuse clinics. The U. S. government pays the money it would have spent running these to the tribe. Chief Mankiller points out that Indians want the maximum of control over their own lives: "I am proud," she says, "to watch my people improve their individual lives on their own through various educational and employment opportunities."[57]

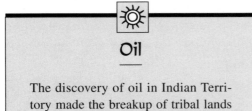

Oil

The discovery of oil in Indian Territory made the breakup of tribal lands more frantic. The first oil was found in the Cherokee Nation, and by 1907 there were 4,366 oil and gas leases in effect in the whole territory. A deep oil field had been found along the western boundary of the Cherokee Nation. The Nation decided that oil rights should be given out to individual owners of the land, and a rush developed. Grafters started offering houses free to oil-land owners to get drilling rights. A few Indians got rich; but many more drillers took away big profits.

The employment opportunities include more than traditional crafts or taking one of the thirteen hundred jobs with the tribe at the Tahlequah headquarters. The Cherokee Nation also owns businesses, including a large factory near Stilwell where electrical wires and cables are made for space-age vehicles. The tribe's greatest moneymaker to date, however, is its bingo business. Three separate facilities rake in millions of dollars yearly for the tribe.

The money goes for everything from protecting the environment to new housing, but a major item is education. The tribe sponsors Sequoyah High School and backs a variety of other educational programs. The Cherokee language in its written and spoken forms has become a symbol of the life of the tribe. At a time when television reaches even the most remote house, the Cherokee language could easily die out; yet those who still speak it are tireless in promoting it. In 1995 and again in 1999, the tribe elected a bilingual leader, Joe Byrd, as Principal Chief to follow Wilma Mankiller.

The tribal government does have its critics. One group of dissenters, the United Keetoowah Band, has received official government recognition (it does not include members of the traditional Keetoowah Society). The complaints are old ones: that the officials of the Nation only want to take on white ways and make money, and that they forget the deep meaning of Cherokee culture. Traditionalists, however, are still able to take part in ceremonies at stomp dance grounds, to hear the old stories in homes and churches, to find

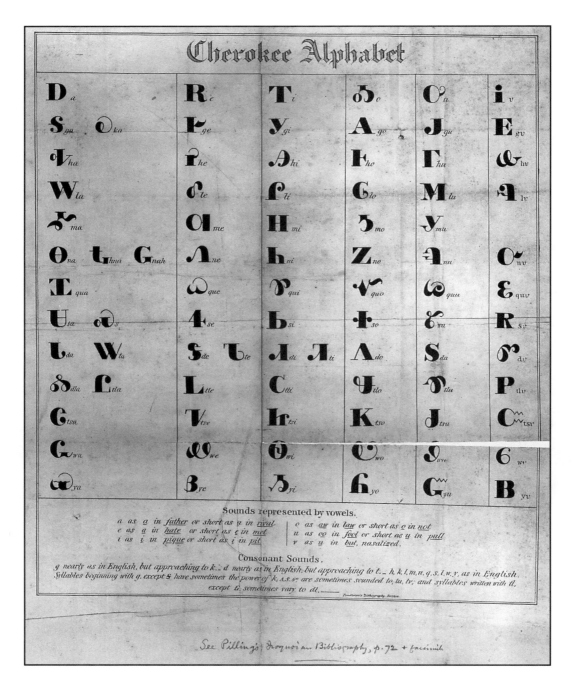

The Cherokee alphabet is still in use today.

The Cherokee keep their culture alive through ceremonies and religious dances.

imported souvenirs. Actors in war bonnets pose for photos next to tepees in scenes taken from movies about Plains Indians, and far from authentic Cherokee culture.

Yet it is not difficult in this town to find beautifully made real Cherokee arts and crafts, both traditional and modern. It is possible to hear storytellers retell old myths and produce new tales, as Native American storytellers have always done. And, away from the main street, it is possible to hear about the Cherokee who still strip witch hazel bark for medicinal tea or meet in a field for a stickball game. The tourist business is a moneymaking enterprise, not a key to the nature of the people. As in Oklahoma, bingo has proven to be another solid moneymaker. It has become the winter employment for Eastern Band members while tourism fills in the summer.

healers who remember old herbal recipes. And, if anyone forgets the recipe or the story, they can stop by the Cherokee National Historical Society and look it up.

Coming Full Circle

The Eastern Band remains tiny compared to the membership in the Cherokee Nation. Yet its long, unbroken life in the Cherokee homeland makes it an important link for all Cherokee. That link may seem hard to find for visitors coming through the town of Cherokee in midsummer. Neon signs point to shops full of junky,

In 1984, an important event took place for all Cherokee. The scene was Red Clay, Tennessee—the starting point for the Trail of Tears. There, the Eastern Band and the Cherokee Nation held the first joint council meeting in history. Ever since, they have met every two years. Their coming together again marks a full circle. It is a sign of new growth and unity that may help wipe away some of the tears of the past for the Cherokee as they face the future.

Being Cherokee in the Future

What will it mean to be Cherokee in the future? Will "Cherokee" become simply a historical label, or will it be an essential part of the lives of the people who bear the name? To answer these questions, it is necessary to know who the Cherokee are now, to consider how they hope to survive, and to put a finger on the deep meaning of being Cherokee.

It Takes a Cherokee Grandmother

From the beginning, the Cherokee were willing to expand the definition of their people to include those they married and those they adopted. The custom has led to perhaps the most mixed and intermarried tribe in the United States. It is interesting to note that many people who identified themselves as Cherokee in censuses of 1990 and 1980 had not done so before. Even more claim some Cherokee heritage. Scholar Russell Thornton points out that, in accord with the tradition of tracing ancestry through the mother's line, "It is not surprising that a large number of non-American Indians—white and black alike—have a 'Cherokee grandmother.' They seem proud of it, and so they should be."[58]

At times in Cherokee history, the more assimilated Cherokee have gained ground at the expense of the more traditional. Yet historians of the tribe argue also that a wide definition of "Cherokee" has allowed the people to take full advantage of the power and sympathy of all those connected to them. The wide circle has protected the core of traditional life ways practiced by a smaller number. And, even people with little Cherokee blood, living far from the core locations in North Carolina and Oklahoma, can and do take up study of their heritage, visit Cherokee sites, and join clubs like the Cherokee Cultural Society of Houston. The Internet is providing more meeting places for Cherokee of every stripe.

Another twist to Cherokee identity increased at the end of the twentieth century:

a more general connection with Native Americans of all tribes. Dancer Thomas Muskrat of the Eastern Band, for example, creates costumes that include Plains Indian styles. "We mix up our Indian regalia and customs a lot,"[59] he says. Many Cherokee take part in intertribal groups such as the Native American Health Coalition or the Native American Arts Council. Are they diluting their Cherokee character? Maybe, but it is also true that the "traditional" Cherokee borrowed freely from their tribal neighbors and from European Americans. Culture cannot be frozen in time.

The Casino and the Museum

To the members of the Cherokee Nation and the Eastern Band, Cherokee survival is tied closely to economic success and social improvement. For many years, they like other Native Americans, were poor and dependent on the federal government for handouts that only just kept them alive and for services that kept failing. Now, as an Eastern Band leader says, "our goal is self-sufficiency."[60] Top moneymakers, the gambling casinos may continue to pay off in the future, as they have since the mid-1980s. But there are worries. Too much prosperity might cause the federal government to withdraw its protections and supports entirely. State governments or other tribes could steal customers away with competitive casinos. Both eastern and western Cherokee have thought of these possibilities and made some plans. Ross Swimmer, head of Cherokee Nation Industries,

says he tells the bingo manager, "Just be sure, if you build any more of those bingo halls, that you build them so I can put a manufacturing business in there after the competition pulls the rug out from under you."[61]

But should the Cherokee be trying to survive in the same way any corporation survives, or should they concentrate on their own ancient arts? Certainly, the museums, outdoor dramas, and crafts help keep Cherokee memories and bring in money, too. But they are not enough to support the people with dignity. Nor do the Cherokee want to feel like exhibits in a museum as the rest of the world passes by.

Wilma Mankiller has said, "We Cherokees have managed to figure out how to live successfully in a very modern, fast-paced world, while preserving our cultural values and traditions."[62] That claim may be optimistic. Young Cherokee are sometimes more enthralled by basketball than by stickball. They prefer McDonald's to bean bread. How can the old ways of the tribe attract them?

Back at the Stomp Ground

One answer can be found at a traditional stomp ground. There, teenagers mix with the very young, the very old, and others in between. People join the dance and wind around and around the central fire. The sense of belonging this ritual gives the participants is fiercely strong and unforgettable.

Other aspects of Cherokee values and traditions can be seen to fit well with some modern thinking. In medicine, for example,

A modern Cherokee woman uses traditional methods to make pots useful for cooking or selling to tourists.

the Cherokee have long recognized that a person's state of mind can be as important to healing as the right drug or herb. Like other Native Americans, the Cherokee have traditionally respected the earth and its plants and animals. The elders teach the importance of slowing down in the fast pace of life, listening to others, attending to the world around you, and making decisions with care. Any modern young Cherokee could benefit from these traditions.

For most Cherokee, their identity as members of the tribe is largely a family matter. It has to do with the traditional support that family members offer one another, the stories and history they retell, and the part they play in the community. Family, clan, and community, with the deep memories they preserve, have helped the tribe rebuild and survive many times in the past. It seems likely that they will continue to do so in times to come.

Notes

Introduction: At the Stomp Ground
1. Wilma Mankiller and Michael Wallis, *Mankiller: A Chief and Her People.* New York: St. Martin's Press, 1993, p. xix.

Chapter 1: Traditional Life in the Mountains
2. Christopher Camuto, *Another Country: Journeying Toward the Cherokee Mountains.* New York: Henry Holt, 1997, p. 78.
3. Quoted in Mankiller and Wallis, *Mankiller,* p. 232.
4. Quoted in Mankiller and Wallis, *Mankiller,* p. 31.
5. Quoted in Theda Perdue, *Cherokee Women: Gender and Culture Change, 1700–1835.* Lincoln: University of Nebraska Press, 1998, p. 18.
6. Quoted in Perdue, *Cherokee Women,* p. 22.
7. Quoted in W. S. Penn, ed., *The Telling of the World: Native American Stories and Art.* New York: Stewart, Tabori, and Chang, 1996, pp. 38–39.

Chapter 2: Belief and Community
8. Quoted in Center for the Electronic Reconstruction of Historical and Archaeological Sites, *EarthWorks: Ancient Newark, Ohio* (videotape). Cincinnati: University of Cincinnati, 1998.
9. Quoted in Alan Kilpatrick, *The Night Has a Naked Soul: Witchcraft and Sorcery Among the Western Cherokee.* Syracuse, NY: Syracuse University Press, 1997, p. 9.
10. Kilpatrick, *The Night Has a Naked Soul,* p. 11.
11. Frank G. Speck and Leonard Broom in collaboration with Will West Long, *Cherokee Dance and Drama.* Norman: University of Oklahoma Press, 1957, pp. 44–45.
12. Quoted in Perdue, *Cherokee Women,* p. 55.
13. Charles Hudson, *The Southeastern Indians.* Knoxville: University of Tennessee Press, 1976, p. 224.
14. Freeman Owle, "The Nikwasi Mound," in Barbara R. Duncan, ed., *Living Stories of the Cherokee.* Chapel Hill: University of North Carolina Press, 1998, p. 201.

Chapter 3: The "Civilization" of the Cherokee
15. Quoted in Edward Gaylord Bourne, ed., *Narratives of the Career of Hernado de Soto.* New York: Allerton Book Co., 1922, p. 71.
16. Quoted in Russell Thornton, *The Cherokees: A Population History.* Lincoln: University of Nebraska Press, 1990, p. 29.

17. Quoted in Perdue, *Cherokee Women,* p. 85.

18. Quoted in Perdue, *Cherokee Women,* p. 66.

19. Quoted in Thornton, *The Cherokees,* p. 38.

20. Quoted in William G. McLoughlin, *Cherokee Renascence in the New Republic.* Princeton, NJ: Princeton University Press, 1986, p. 37.

21. Quoted in McLoughlin, *Cherokee Renascence in the New Republic,* p. 156.

22. Ruth Bradley Holmes and Betty Sharp Smith, *Beginning Cherokee,* 2nd ed. Norman: University of Oklahoma Press, 1977, p. 293.

23. Quoted in McLoughlin, *Cherokee Renascence in the New Republic,* p. 288.

24. Quoted in McLoughlin, *Cherokee Renascence in the New Republic,* p. 412.

25. Quoted in McLoughlin, *Cherokee Renascence in the New Republic,* p. 435.

26. Quoted in McLoughlin, *Cherokee Renascence in the New Republic,* p. 450.

27. Quoted in Thurman Wilkins, *Cherokee Tragedy: The Ridge Family and the Decimation of a People,* 2nd ed. Norman: University of Oklahoma Press, 1986, p. 289.

Chapter 4: The Trail of Tears

28. Jerry Ellis, *Walking the Trail: One Man's Journey Along the Cherokee Trail of Tears.* New York: Delacorte Press, 1991, p. 245.

29. Quoted in Joan Gilbert, *The Trail of Tears Across Missouri.* Columbia: University of Missouri Press, 1996, p. 23.

30. Quoted in Duane H. King, "The Origin of the Eastern Cherokees as a Social and Political Entity," in Duane H. King, ed. *The Cherokee Indian Nation: A Troubled History.* Knoxville: University of Tennessee Press, 1979, p. 169.

31. Quoted in Thornton, *The Cherokees,* p. 65.

32. Quoted in Thornton, *The Cherokees,* pp. 65–66.

33. Quoted in Thornton, *The Cherokees,* p. 66.

34. Freeman Owle, "The Trail of Tears," in Duncan, ed., *Living Stories of the Cherokee,* p. 222.

35. Quoted in Thornton, *The Cherokees,* p. 68.

36. Quoted in Thornton, *The Cherokees,* p. 71.

37. Quoted in Grant Foreman, *Indian Removal: The Emigration of the Five Civilized Tribes of Indians.* Norman: University of Oklahoma Press, 1932, p. 305.

38. Quoted in Foreman, *Indian Removal,* p. 303.

39. Quoted in Gilbert, *The Trail of Tears Across Missouri,* p. 47.

40. Quoted in Gilbert, *The Trail of Tears Across Missouri,* p. 57.

41. Quoted in Foreman, *Indian Removal,* p. 309.

Chapter 5: In the New Lands

42. Quoted in Wilkins, *Cherokee Tragedy,* p. 310.

43. Quoted in Theda Perdue, *Slavery and*

the Evolution of Cherokee Society. Knoxville: University of Tennessee Press, 1979, p. 75.

44. Quoted in Gerard Reed, "Postremoval Factionalism in the Cherokee Nation," in King, ed., *The Cherokee Indian Nation,* p. 160.

45. Quoted in William G. McLoughlin, *After the Trail of Tears: The Cherokees' Struggle for Sovereignty, 1839–1880.* Chapel Hill: University of North Carolina Press, 1993, p. 37.

46. Quoted in McLoughlin, *After the Trail of Tears,* p. 76.

47. Quoted in McLoughlin, *After the Trail of Tears,* p. 157.

48. Quoted in McLoughlin, *After the Trail of Tears,* p. 183.

49. Quoted in Thornton, *The Cherokees,* p. 94.

50. Quoted in McLoughlin, *After the Trail of Tears,* p. 257.

51. Quoted in McLoughlin, *After the Trail of Tears,* p. 272.

52. Quoted in Mankiller and Wallis, *Mankiller,* pp. 133–34.

Chapter 6: Twentieth-Century Cherokee

53. Quoted in Angie Debo, *And Still the Waters Run: The Betrayal of the Five Civilized Tribes.* Princeton, NJ: Princeton University Press, 1940. Reprint, Norman: University of Oklahoma Press, 1972, pp. 27-28.

54. Debo, *And Still the Waters Run,* p. 91.

55. Quoted in Debo, *And Still the Waters Run,* p. 153.

56. Quoted in King, *The Cherokee Indian Nation,* p. 239.

57. Mankiller and Wallis, *Mankiller,* p. 254.

Epilogue: Being Cherokee in the Future

58. Thornton, *The Cherokees,* p. 171.

59. Quoted in Geoffrey Norman, "The Cherokee: Two Nations, One People," *National Geographic,* May 1995, p. 95.

60. Quoted in Norman, "The Cherokee: Two Nations, One People," p. 83.

61. Quoted in Norman, "The Cherokee: Two Nations, One People," p. 93.

62. Mankiller and Wallis, *Mankiller,* p. 254.

For Further Reading

Books

Marlene Targ Brill, *The Trail of Tears: The Cherokee Journey from Home.* Brookfield, CT: Millbrook, 1995. A brief account of the Cherokee removal, with useful maps.

Barbara R. Duncan, ed., *Living Stories of the Cherokee.* Chapel Hill: University of North Carolina Press, 1998. Presents lively recorded stories by six contemporary North Carolina Cherokee, including both traditional myths and personal memories and experiences; includes a very helpful introduction about this living literature.

Rodney L. Leftwich, *Arts and Crafts of the Cherokee.* Cherokee, NC: Cherokee Publications, 1970. This book is a thorough introduction to Cherokee basket making, pottery, sculpture, etc., with many photographs and remarks by living Cherokee artists.

James Mooney, *Cherokee Animal Tales.* Ed. George F. Scheer. New York: Holiday House, 1968. This is a small selection of the Cherokee myths originally collected by James Mooney from the Cherokee in the 1890s.

Jane Shumate, *Sequoyah: Inventor of the Cherokee Alphabet.* New York: Chelsea House, 1994. The full story of Sequoyah's life, which included much more than the alphabet; with illustrations.

Donald Sizemore, *How to Make Cherokee Clothing.* Cherokee, NC: Cherokee Publications, 1995. This fun book tells how to make Cherokee-style clothing from materials generally available today, and includes fascinating descriptions of Cherokee garments and decorations.

Della A. Yannuzzi, *Wilma Mankiller: Leader of the Cherokee Nation.* Hillside, NJ: Enslow, 1994. This biography of Wilma Mankiller shows her extraordinary achievement in spite of many disadvantages and physical problems.

Periodicals, Videos, and Websites

Jim Berger, executive producer, *How the West Was Lost II* (video-recording). Bethesda, MD: Discovery Enterprises Group, 1995. Volumes two and three of this superb documentary tell the story of the Trail of Tears and the loss of Cherokee land at the end of the nineteenth century, with voices of Cherokee people from today and from the past.

Geoffrey Norman, "The Cherokee: Two Nations, One People," *National Geographic,* May 1995. This article gives an excellent overview of Cherokee life today in Oklahoma and North Carolina.

(www.cherokee.org) This is the website of the official Cherokee Nation in Oklahoma. It includes news and pictures, some from the tribe's newspaper, the *Cherokee Advocate and Phoenix.*

(www.cherokee-nc.com) This website of the Eastern Band contains information about cultural events, genealogy, and more. It is generally meant for visitors rather than Band members.

Works Consulted

Edward Gaylord Bourne, ed., *Narratives of the Career of Hernando de Soto*. New York: Allerton, 1922. This is a collection of on-the-spot records and "histories" of De Soto's progress through the Southeast in 1540, full of fascinating detail and bizarre encounters between the Spanish and Native Americans.

Christopher Camuto, *Another Country: Journeying Toward the Cherokee Mountains*. New York: Henry Holt, 1997. A beautifully written personal narrative about walking solo in ancient Cherokee country, with the story of the reintroduction of wolves into that wilderness.

Center for the Electronic Reconstruction of Historical and Archaeological Sites, *EarthWorks: Ancient Newark, Ohio* (videotape). Cincinnati: University of Cincinnati, 1998. This brief video documentary suggests possible meanings of prehistoric mound architecture in terms of some early Native American myths.

Angie Debo, *And Still the Waters Run: The Betrayal of the Five Civilized Tribes*. Princeton, NJ: Princeton University Press, 1940. Reprint, Norman: University of Oklahoma Press, 1972. The story of the allotment of land in the 1890s, in very full and scholarly detail with telling quotations from congressional hearings.

Jerry Ellis, *Walking the Trail: One Man's Journey Along the Cherokee Trail of Tears*. New York: Delacorte Press, 1991. The journal of a contemporary man of Cherokee heritage, reacting to some places and events of the Cherokee removal.

John R. Finger, *Cherokee Americans: The Eastern Band of Cherokees in the Twentieth Century*. Lincoln: University of Nebraska Press, 1991. A thorough account of Eastern Band social and economic life since 1900.

Grant Foreman, *Indian Removal: The Emigration of the Five Civilized Tribes of Indians*. Norman: University of Oklahoma Press, 1932. This detailed history recounts the experience of the Cherokee and other southeast Indian tribes along the Trail of Tears.

Joan Gilbert, *The Trail of Tears Across Missouri.* Columbia: University of Missouri Press, 1996. A clear and moving story of the trek across Missouri with many first-person accounts; written for general readers.

Ruth Bradley Holmes and Betty Sharp Smith, *Beginning Cherokee.* 2nd ed. Norman: University of Oklahoma Press, 1977. This is a Cherokee language textbook, but supplementary essays and explanations in the lessons tell about special qualities of the language, plus some Cherokee history.

Charles Hudson, *The Southeastern Indians.* Knoxville: University of Tennessee Press, 1976. A thorough but lively account of the culture of the Cherokee and their southeastern Indian neighbors; the author pulls together as much evidence as possible of what life was like before the arrival of Europeans.

Alan Kilpatrick, *The Night Has a Naked Soul: Witchcraft and Sorcery Among the Western Cherokee.* Syracuse, NY: Syracuse University Press, 1997. Presents a set of previously unpublished Cherokee magical texts, and includes a good essay on the activities of witches and priests.

Duane H. King, ed., *The Cherokee Indian Nation: A Troubled History.* Knoxville: University of Tennessee Press, 1979. A collection of essays on many aspects of Cherokee history, including Cherokee origins.

Thomas E. Mails, *The Cherokee People: The Story of the Cherokees from Earliest Origins to Contemporary Times.* Tulsa: Council Oak Books, 1992. This book is especially valuable for the many drawings of early Cherokee objects and dress, based on an old manuscript prepared from interviews with tribe members in the 1830s.

Wilma Mankiller and Michael Wallis, *Mankiller: A Chief and Her People.* New York: St. Martin's Press, 1993. In this full-length autobiography, Principal Chief Mankiller details her life from activism in California to a return to her Cherokee roots in Oklahoma.

William G. McLoughlin, *After the Trail of Tears: The Cherokees' Struggle for Sovereignty, 1839–1880.* Chapel Hill: University of North Carolina Press, 1993. This is the highly detailed, authoritative history of this period.

————, *Cherokee Renascence in the New Republic.* Princeton, NJ: Princeton University Press, 1986. The author brings an objective viewpoint and great mastery of historic detail to the story of the Cherokee's development between 1783 and 1835.

W. S. Penn, ed., *The Telling of the World: Native American Stories and Art.* New York: Stewart, Tabori, and Chang, 1996. This large, beautiful book includes stories about the origins of people and things from many different tribes, with illustrations from ancient and modern Native American artists.

Theda Perdue, *Cherokee Women: Gender and Culture Change, 1700–1835.* Lincoln: University of Nebraska Press, 1998. The story of the price Cherokee women paid for "civilization," told in scholarly style with fascinating attention to the real nature of female lives.

————, *Slavery and the Evolution of Cherokee Society.* Knoxville: University of Tennessee Press, 1979. This book thoroughly explains the whys and wherefores of slavery as practiced by the Cherokee.

Theda Perdue and Michael D. Green, eds., *The Cherokee Removal: A Brief History with Documents.* Boston: Bedford Books, 1995. A readable collection of thought-provoking documents and accounts from the Trail of Tears.

Ralph and Lisa Woo Shanks, *The North American Indian Travel Guide.* Petaluma, CA: Castano Books, 1996. This travel guide includes Cherokee sites open to the public in North Carolina, Oklahoma, and elsewhere.

Frank G. Speck and Leonard Broom in collaboration with Will West Long, *Cherokee Dance and Drama.* Norman: University of Oklahoma Press, 1957. Includes descriptions and diagrams of many traditional Cherokee dances, with commentary.

Renard Strickland, *Fire and the Spirits: Cherokee Law from Clan to Court.* Norman: University of Oklahoma Press, 1975. This book explains how Cherokee laws and trials mixed American customs and Cherokee traditional practices.

Russell Thornton, *The Cherokees: A Population History.* Lincoln: University of Nebraska Press, 1990. The author traces the changing numbers and the changing definitions of the Cherokee from before Columbus to the present.

Thurman Wilkins, *Cherokee Tragedy: The Ridge Family and the Decimation of a People.* 2nd ed. Norman: University of Oklahoma Press, 1986. This long and dramatic book tells the side of the pro-Removal Party in the years leading up to the Trail of Tears.

Index

Picture Credits

Cover photo: Corbis/Bettmann
AP/Wide World Photos, 74
Corbis, 65
Corbis/Zandria Muench Beraldo, 10
Corbis/Bettmann, 39, 67
Corbis/Kevin Fleming, 77
Corbis/Raymond Gehman, 72
Corbis/Medford Historical Society Collection, 57
Corbis/Tim Thompson, 20
Corbis/Peter Turnley, 7
Gilcrease Museum/Brummet Echohawk, 46
Library of Congress, 40, 42, 43, 61, 64, 76
Museum of the Cherokee Indian, 12, 16, 19, 24, 27, 52, 69, 80
North Wind Picture Archives, 30, 35
Stock Montage, 68
The Woolaroc Museum/Robert Lindneux, 54

About the Author

Cathryn J. Long studied English literature at the University of California, Berkeley, where she received her undergraduate degree and did graduate work. She has written a variety of books for students and others in fields of world affairs and history. Local history in and around the Ohio Valley is a special interest: She has written a play for students about Cincinnati at the turn of the century, authored a billboard display of river history at the Ohio River Tallstacks event, and written an Ohio history for young people. She is currently at work on a University of Cincinnati sponsored project which allows people to visit prehistoric Indian earthworks and mounds through a computer-generated landscape. Long lives in Cincinnati with her husband and two children. She likes to read, make music with friends, and explore historic sites.